John Bickerdyke

Days in Thule with rod, gun and camera

John Bickerdyke

Days in Thule with rod, gun and camera

ISBN/EAN: 9783337198121

Printed in Europe, USA, Canada, Australia, Japan

Cover: Foto ©Andreas Hilbeck / pixelio.de

More available books at **www.hansebooks.com**

DAYS IN THULE

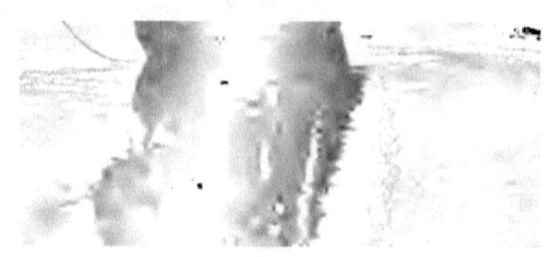

DAYS IN THULE

WITH ROD, GUN, AND CAMERA

BY

JOHN BICKERDYKE

AUTHOR OF 'A BANISHED BEAUTY,' 'THE BOOK OF
THE ALL-ROUND ANGLER,' 'THAMES RIGHTS
AND THAMES WRONGS,' 'THE CURIOSITIES
OF ALE AND BEER,' ETC.

WITH NUMEROUS ILLUSTRATIONS

Westminster
ARCH. CONSTABLE AND CO.
14 PARLIAMENT ST. S.W.
MDCCCXCIV

Edinburgh: T. and A. CONSTABLE, Printers to Her Majesty

DEDICATO ALLA MIA GRAZIOSISSIMA
E GENTILISSIMA OSPITE

CLOTILDE

IN MEMORIA DEI FELICISSIMI GIORNI
PASSATI NELLE CONTRADE
DESERTE DEL NORD

PREFACE

THE foundations of this book were laid in the columns of the *Field* and *Graphic*, and I have much pleasure in gratefully acknowledging the courtesy shown me by the editors of these admirable journals. I have added several stories to the little edifice, have remodelled and planned, decorated, inside and out, roofed in, and now offer the result to the critical gaze of the reading public.

This is a simple record of life in a Hebridean shooting-lodge. If any one who has done me the honour to read the adventures of *A Banished*

Beauty in a somewhat similar locality should find here and there points of slight resemblance in some description of scenery or sporting incident, I beg him remember that in the writing of novels, as in the spinning of anglers' yarns, an occasional lapse into truth is desirable to give the effect of realism. At the same time let me hasten with all possible speed to say, that it was not at Gheira Lodge I made the acquaintance of those three remarkable Cockney sportsmen who figure in the work of fiction. What we really did, and how we did it, is herein more or less truthfully described, with some slight change of names, which was obviously desirable.

I may, perhaps, be taken to task for not giving more information concerning the habits of the people of Lewis and the management of the island. That portion of the subject has been so

PREFACE

fully dealt with by Mr. Anderson Smith, in *Lewsiana*, a book to be read by every one who visits the island, that there was little or nothing for me to add.

JOHN BICKERDYKE.

SOUTH STOKE, OXON,
June 1894.

Amateur photographers may, perhaps, be interested to know that the illustrations, with the exception of those on pages 2, 92, 125, 149, and 177, are due to the more or less judicious manipulation of a $\frac{1}{4}$-plate Kodak.

CONTENTS

CHAP.		PAGE
I.	GHEIRA LODGE,	1
II.	THE HADDIES OF THULE,	15
III.	WILD DOGS AND TAME GROUSE,	28
IV.	CONJURING SALMON,	43
V.	DUCK, PLOVER, AND SNIPE,	59
VI.	A SULKY SALMON AND A GREEDY COD,	69
VII.	AN ASSAULT ON THE BLUE ROCK STRONGHOLDS	82
VIII.	THREE LOCHS AND A PUDDLE,	100
IX.	'SALMO IRRITANS' AND HIS VANQUISHMENT,	115
X.	THE RABBITS OF THE CLIFFS,	141
XI.	OUR SEA-TROUT DITCH,	157
XII.	FAREWELL TO THULE,	168

ILLUSTRATIONS

	PAGE
FRONTISPIECE.	
'A BUILDING KNOWN ALL OVER THE KINGDOM AS "THE CASTLE,"'	2
'IT IS PITIFUL, IS IT NOT?'	7
'A FERRY-BOAT CRAMMED WITH PEOPLE,'	17
'BOATS NEED BE WEATHERLY THERE,'	18
'WE PAY AN EARLY VISIT TO THE KENNELS,'	29
'A PIOUS OLD WOMAN,'	33
'DID I EFFER POACH A SAUMON?—OH, AY!'	53
'BLACK, UNFERTILE, DESOLATE-LOOKING PLACES,'	64
'HE SAT ON THE BANK COMPLACENTLY SMOKING,'	75
'THE SHELTERED NOOK WHERE SOME HERRING-BOATS LAY AT ANCHOR,'	86
'I WAS ABLE TO OPEN THE LENS AT THE VERY MOMENT ONE OF THOSE WHO WERE ON BOARD FIRED,'	92
'THE ONE OCCASION ON WHICH I MADE HIM LAUGH OUTRIGHT,'	103

DAYS IN THULE

	PAGE
'THEY DO LOOK AS IF THEY WERE DANCING A WILD JIG, DON'T THEY?'	122
'SOMETHING SPECIALLY DIABOLICAL,'	125
'A LITTLE MATTER OF TWENTY-TWO MILES THERE AND HOME AGAIN!'	144
'A PICTURESQUE GROUP,'	145
'SURF BREAKING ON THE SAND, BUT NO SEAL,'	149
'SHE'S JOOST A FINE MARE,' HE WAS SAYING,	161
'FRITH TOOK A PHOTO OF ONE LITTLE ROADSIDE SCENE,'	177
SKYE,	179
'BOUND FOR OBAN AND CIVILISATION,'	181

CHAPTER I

GHEIRA LODGE

 'STRANGE land.'

My three days' journey down the Clyde and abreast the beautiful west coast of Scotland had come to an end at Stornoway, which, like Dublin, rejoices in a building known all over the kingdom as 'the castle.' The herring-scented little capital was a mile or more astern of the dog-cart, and a sturdy grey pony, jerked along by an equally sturdy, thickset, powerful man, was drawing me rapidly over the moorland road which skirted Broad Bay, choicest haddock-ground, not only of the Outer Hebrides, but of all Scotland.

DAYS IN THULE

'A strange land indeed.'

As I made the remark, more to myself than Donald, we were passing through the 'black

'A BUILDING KNOWN ALL OVER THE KINGDOM AS "THE CASTLE.

country' of the Lewis, the great peat-bogs, whence the little capital of the island draws its chief supplies of fuel. Any slight traces of vegetation there may have been were hidden by the gathering twilight. All round us the country was dark and gloomy, its monotony only varied by heaps of black peat stacked ready for cart or creel. The scene was weird, almost horrible; a fitting abode for witches and uncanny things. Even in sunlight it was not a cheerful place. Was this the beautiful Thule I had read of? It seemed to me rather the abomination of desolation.

Soon, with much clatter, we crossed a rickety, wooden bridge.

'The Creedy,' said Donald.

'Salmon?' I queried.

'It is the fourth best river in the island.'

The country changed now, and we came to the sweet, open, undulating moorland, untouched, save by the grazing of crofters' cows and the trimming of the heather tops by the grouse. Not a tree nor any sign of life was visible; not even a stone wall. The long white road and a fishing-boat in the bay were the only signs of civilisation. Another mile was left behind us, and I made out, on the low-lying land towards the sea, a long double row of round-topped, badly-thatched ricks.

'That is Vashka,' said Donald.

'A big farmer,' said I, 'to have all those ricks.'

Donald's grave intelligent face bore an amused expression. 'They are no ricks, whateffer, they are crofters' cottages.'

Imagine a building more or less rectangular, but with rounded ends, the walls low and immensely thick, some faced, inside and out, with unhewn and unmortared stones—earth or peat lying between, others built entirely of peat sods. On the top of this wall, a flat grassy walk whereon children play, goats feed, and clothes and nets are placed to dry. A round, low, eaveless roof rising from the inner edges of the four walls, the thatch being held in place by hay or straw bands stretched tightly across, and sometimes by an old herring net. The whole often windowless, always chimneyless. Imagine this, if you can, and you

GHEIRA LODGE

have in your mind's eye a Hebridean cot, such perhaps as has been built any time these past five hundred years, and differing not greatly from the ancient bee-hive dwelling.

Donald told me many things of the primitive, good-natured, God-fearing, landlord-hating folk who constructed those curious tenements. Chimneys they abhorred; the wise people of Thule having long ago discovered that smoke contained something which was good for the land. Each year, therefore, their well-charged smoke-filters went on to their crofts and added to the crops of the next. In other words, once in every twelve months the thatch, saturated with smoke, was stripped from the roofs and spread over the fields, fresh straw taking its place. So short was the straw, owing to the all too short summers, that some of the grain crops were usually pulled up by the roots. That little, which would have constituted stubble if the crop had been reaped, could not be spared by these poor but thrifty people.

DAYS IN THULE

A chimneyless room in Peatland is not so very horrible a place. The fire, a heap of live peats, smoulders as often as not in the centre of the clay floor, and the white smoke rises upwards and collects in the round roof where the chickens roost on the odds and ends of drift-wood, which support the thatch. After curling awhile among the poultry it filters out through the thick thatch.

Those who sit on the low bench by the fire smell the peat reek, but do not choke of it. Weak eyes smart a little just at first, that is all, and in compensation the pleasant peat bouquet overcomes less pleasant odours, and seems to kill the germs of fever and some other diseases. I smiled (somewhat sadly) at first sight of those strange miserable-looking dwellings, but later on I understood how in that land of violent winds and heavy rains walls had to be thick and roofs eaveless. No jerry-built villa nor model cottage could withstand the weather on those wind-swept, water-worn moors.

GHEIRA LODGE

But still, look at the piled-up stones with heap of barley roots on top, which is shown in the illustration. That aperture is the entrance to a

'IT IS PITIFUL, IS IT NOT?'

fellow-creature's home. It is pitiful, is it not? There two—perhaps three—generations of a family dwell; winter and summer, storm and fair, wet or dry. Children are born in it, old men and women die in it, cattle are stabled in it the winter through. My lords and gentlemen, when you talk harshly or think unkindly of these people, because, may be, they lack sympathy with your sports, or are in arrears with rents, remember their surroundings, and that to them are given none of the cakes and ale of this life. Their manly endurance is heroic almost, but if sometimes discontent comes bubbling up to the surface and a cry is raised for more land or better houses, who are we that we should cast stones? Who is content? And echo answers quickly.

Some such thoughts as these flitted involuntarily through my mind as we drove rapidly past the squalid clachan.

The whole country told in its face a story of wild winter weather. The hillsides were seamed with numberless furrows cut right down through the thick layer of peat to the hard rock beneath. Long tangled mosses, beautiful but deadly, choked the clumps of heather on the moist parts of the moor. The heather was shorter and less luxuriant than any I had seen elsewhere. Lochs and streams were everywhere, burns often sinking into the moorland in places and rising to sight again lower down the valleys nearer the sea. And there were no trees: that told a tale.

Leaving Vashka and another village behind us, we passed a few acres of enclosed grass-land surrounding a substantial stone house—one of the small sheep farms which have wholly, or in part, been made on land originally reclaimed from the moor by the crofters. Then we journeyed through more moorland, rumbled over the wooden bridge which spanned the salmon-river of my host, and trotted through great bent-covered sand-hills. Among these lay an ancient unfenced burying-place, the forefathers of the clan taking their last sleep round the ruins of a venerable chapel. Suddenly the road left the sand-hills, there arose a great barking of dogs, and just as darkness fell I found myself brought in contact with civilisation once more; kennels, stables, keeper's cottage, farm-buildings, shooting-lodge, all grouped around, a blaze of light coming from an open door, and two genial-looking women beaming on the new arrival.

It was not until the following morning that I learned how beautiful was the spot in which I was to spend the summer and early autumn of 189-. Great Broad Bay, fringed with miles of dazzling white sands, lay before us, and dimly in the distance we could see the blue mountains of Skye and the mainland. The lodge was built on the very edge of the sand-dunes. So close, indeed, were we to the sea, that a former tenant once shot an unsuspecting grebe from an upper window. It happened during a spring tide, at high water, and the bird was swimming past close to the shore.

A quarter of a mile or so from us were two barren islands, where gulls, curlew, geese, divers and sundry wild-fowl met in conclave and held animated conversations. Sheltered by the islets and cliffs which rose gradually to the northward, lay black-hulled fishing-boats at anchor in the bay. Behind us to the westward stretched away miles of warm, brown moorland, purpled here and there by the heather just bursting into blossom, and rising gradually to the horizon where Ben Mo-nach, with his twin tops, stood not grandly, but rather stolidly out against the gorgeous northern sunsets.

Six or seven miles to the southward, and forming one side of the great bay, was that curious strip of land known as the 'Eye of Lewis,' at the end of which—it pleased me to remember—the old King of Borva viewed out of sight the steamer which was bearing away his darling Sheila, Princess of Thule. Further southward still rose the mountains of Harris, and rarely was it that their summits were not cloud-capped. Ever-changing sea, heather-covered moorlands, rugged mountains, silvery sands, gorgeous atmospheric effects—what more could man wish?

I cannot answer for man in the abstract, but I confess that the individuals then dwelling in Gheira Lodge *had* desires even beyond these things. They thought much, for instance, of grouse, salmon, and trout, and felt, moreover, an interest in such smaller items as plover, blue hares, rabbit, blue rock-pigeons, duck, and wildfowl generally. I, in addition, had visions of great hauls of sea-fish, and even the ladies of our party, having heard legends of enormous mushrooms, were anxious to roam those grassy slopes near the cliffs. Later on their fair ambition took the form of burn-trout, rising gradually through loch-trout and sea-trout to salmon.

Happy times had we in this nook of Britain, but let it be understood that there were days when fish would not rise, or scent was bad, or rain would not come; days on which the heart of the average British sportsman was apt to get sad, and was not to be cheered by the grandest scenery, or nature's greatest efforts with cloud, mist, sunshine, and vapour. How well I remember one weary, wet drag of many miles over the moor to certain distant lochs after wildfowl! We killed one duck, lost our way, and one of our party was made ill by over-exertion!

Did we not on another memorable occasion for many hours stalk great flocks of shy, plump, tasty, golden plover, five guns killing one bird between them? Were not miles of water often fished without a rise from a salmon? Such fortune may befall one anywhere occasionally; I only raise up the ghosts of such evil times to prevent misleading those of my readers who might otherwise think that among Hebridean roses there were no thorns. More than once has the published description of some red-letter day with rod or gun lured me to undertake some long and expensive expedition, only to find at the end of it that either the description I had read was of sport enjoyed years ago (when things were different), or during an exceptional visitation of beast or fish. Sometimes, too, in my experience, it has happened that glowing descriptions of sport have been untrue from beginning to end, having been written to bring visitors to some hotel, or to effect the letting of moor or salmon-river.

May I venture to offer a word of advice before closing this chapter? Never rent a moor or a stream without first having a written list of the game and fish killed the previous year, and the number of guns and rods which were brought into action to make the bag. If possible, verify the list by a reference to the last tenant. If no list was kept, be certain that few birds or fish were killed. A well-known agent once pressed upon me a salmon-river, where on inquiry I found that the average take was four fish a year. In the previous season only one salmon had been killed! Ascertain, too, when the river is at its best. It is poor comfort after renting a river for the spring months to be told that there will be a grand run of fish in July.

CHAPTER II

THE HADDIES OF THULE

THERE was dead low water in the salmon-river, and no breeze for the lochs. The shooting-season proper had not commenced. Thus it came about that four individuals in search of an occupation had to fall back upon such sport as the sea might afford; the sea at that particular spot being, as I have already said, represented by Broad Bay, the most notable haddock-ground in the kingdom.

If lying among the sand-dunes, lazily watching the sea-birds and drinking deep draughts of that glorious, exhilarating, health-giving, Hebridean air can be deemed a waste of time, which I very much doubt, we wasted the morning as one is very apt to do in hot summer weather. But Murdo the Black and Murdo the Long searched meanwhile for mussels with good effect, and got the boat ready. Inattention to detail is a peculiarity of the Celtic races, and had been exemplified on former sea-fishing excursions by a rope hardly long enough to reach the bottom, an anchor all too small to hold our little craft in a breeze, and a recklessness in the matter of putting the boat on the marks, which accounted for poor sport on previous expeditions of the kind.

But to-day we were properly found. When in Stornoway I had bought a fine long manilla rope, and the anchor was to be supplemented by one of the large stones which we carried as ballast. Moreover, I had mastered the marks and had made up my mind that we should be brought within a boat's-length of the right spot, Celt or no Celt.

If you would care to see a picture of our little

craft, turn to chapter VII., where you will note that she was put to other uses than fishing. There are many of what one may term local

'A FERRY-BOAT CRAMMED WITH PEOPLE.'

patterns of boats, each being designed to possess just those qualities which are rendered necessary by the peculiarities of the coast. The surf-boats of India, the cobles of the flat, sandy Yorkshire

DAYS IN THULE

shores, which have half a keel, and a flat bottom aft; the deep, stable yacht—why, a long essay might be written on the subject. Coming up the

'BOATS NEED BE WEATHERLY THERE.'

west coast I photographed many an interesting craft from the steamboat. One of them (photograph, not craft) may be seen facing the title-page. Then there was a picture of a ferry-boat

THE HADDIES OF THULE

crammed with people—luggage apparently on the top of the people—a hay-rake of noble proportions over all, and a balk of timber just thrown overboard from the steamer to be towed ashore. Compare this open boat, used in sheltered bays to go short distances between steamer and shore, with the weatherly craft which I saw lying at anchor in Loch Hourn. That loch of precipitous mountain-sides has a death-roll each year of men, for the unexpected mountain wind-rush causes many capsizes. Boats need be weatherly there, for even on the fairest summer day no man who sails those waters in undecked boat may be sure of his life for ten minutes together. Our particular boat has to be fairly flat, for she is beached when not in use, but the Minch is lively at times, so she needs must be a good sea boat, and also sail well. These desirable qualities she has in a greater or less degree, and is probably as well suited to our purpose as anything that could be built. But I am wandering far from Broad

Bay and its excellent haddies. While I have been talking the lug-sail has been hoisted, and we are fairly under weigh.

A light westerly breeze sped us quickly towards the fishing-ground. Getting a derelict fishing-boat, whose ribs were bleaching on the sandy shore, in a line with the top of the highest hill on the land we were leaving, I held my course until an emerald-green patch of sward opened up from behind a black-looking rocky point to the northward. Immediately this appeared the anchor was let go, and the little vessel quickly brought to.

In five minutes our lines were overboard and a second later one of the lady anglers announced with satisfaction that she had caught the first fish, but on pulling up her spreader found she had merely lost her baits, which was not quite the same thing. Then my rod, which I had momentarily put down, all but went overboard, and after a few minutes' play two beautiful haddocks could be seen flashing about in the clear water some

THE HADDIES OF THULE

fathoms beneath the boat. Before these could be landed my friend cried, 'I have one!' and rapidly hauled up a fish of about 2lb. weight. I asked Murdo the Black for the landing-net, whereat he looked at me wonderingly; but Murdo the Long, who was more accustomed to the ways of Englishmen, said the one word 'scumma'—I spell it phonetically—and Murdo the Black understood.

I was fishing, as I do whenever it is possible, with a stout, single gut paternoster, bearing two eyed hooks. In that bay there is but little stream, so light leads can be used, and as the bottom is for the most part sandy, one has a chance of playing and landing a large fish on what is, for the sea, remarkably fine tackle. Rod and line fishing can therefore be followed with comfort, and, moreover, with great advantage, on bright, calm days. Before my fish were out of the landing-net, there was a cry of 'scumma' from the other side of the boat, and while the net was being passed across, it was again wanted on my side. In fact, no sooner was our tackle within a fathom of the bottom than a fish seized the bait, and frequently two were caught on one line.

The Murdos were kept busy taking off the fish and re-baiting the lines, but being polite, as all Highlanders are, devoted themselves principally to the lady anglers, whose excitement was great. In the midst of it all Murdo the Long announced that there were no more mussels, whereat our faces lengthened considerably.

But there is a good providence which occasionally, but not too often, looks after anglers, and the very last mussel produced a grey gurnet of about 1½lb., which cut up into a number of tough and lasting baits. With these we caught haddocks as quickly as with the shell-fish, and the fun continued fast and furious.

Unnoticed by us the wind had freshened a little, and slowly but surely we were dragging our anchor. The remedy, one which salt-water anglers who are not acquainted with the wrinkle may bear in mind with advantage, was to send a messenger down to the anchor, the said messenger being a stone taken from the ballast. A short piece of rope was fastened to it, the ends were loosely tied round the mooring rope, and the stone cast into the sea. In a few seconds it had slid down the mooring rope on to the anchor, and we no longer drifted. In a high wind I have sometimes had as many as three large stones sent down the mooring cable. Care must be taken, however, not to put such a weight on the cable that the anchor plus messengers cannot be weighed without breaking the rope, for a broken cable will in all probability mean a lost anchor.

Finally we left off fishing while the fish were still biting—a sadly improper thing to do, but rendered necessary by our having no bait left but haddocks themselves, slight qualms on the part of one of the ladies, and the near approach of the dinner-hour. It may seem trivial to enter into these details, but to cease fishing in the full tide of success is so remarkable as to require a thorough explanation.

While the men tidied the boat and coiled up the hand-lines we counted the fish, and found we had fifty-five, which weighed considerably over half a hundredweight. How different they looked to the haddock of the fishmonger's shop. They are beautiful fish when first hauled up out of the water, being then a warm grey colour, with a pale mauve bloom over them, and eyes bright and lustrous. I heard a lady, who knew only the shop variety, ask, 'What fish is this?' so great was the difference. Nor is the matter only one of appearance, for the haddock freshly caught is a very superior food to the rather coarse fish which we get in big cities. But then we usually boil them, and if a fish is naturally poor, boiling it is the way to show it at its worst. A boiled haddock is like a picture without a frame. Katie, our Hebridean cook, taught us that the way to cook haddies was to fillet them like soles, egg and bread-crumb, and fry. Thus done, most of those who had the good fortune to taste them preferred them to sea-trout. Never shall I forget those fillets of Broad Bay haddocks.

The wind being off shore and now somewhat light and fitful, we did not beat home. Each with a long sweep—a clumsy apology for an oar, the two Murdos pulled us slowly towards the lodge, we fishers taking their places for the last quarter of a mile. With a rabbit-rifle we vainly attempted to bring down one of the solan geese which were still diligently fishing around us. Twice we managed to send a bullet through the feathers of a bird's wing, but that was all.

Behind the great peat-bog, for Lewis is little else, the sun was going down red into the Atlantic. The blue peat-smoke ascended from the low, thatched, hive-like dwellings of the crofters, and lights shone brightly in some of the windows of the lodge. The excitement of pulling up the fish once over, we found time to discover that even in summer it is owre chilly on the water eight hundred miles north of London. Then came the landing among the slippery rocks, Murdo the Long gallantly carrying the ladies on shore.

Close by our landing-place, on the edge of the sea-weed which fringed the rocks, a salmon and half a dozen sea-trout were leaping—pleasing augury of sport to come in the river when the fish were able to run up. Then there was the picturesque walk back to the lodge by the top of the cliffs over short, sweet grass, the growing-place of certain commendable mushrooms. The Murdos came staggering after us with the fish, and Katie, who had been watching for our arrival, met us at the door all smiles, and pleased as we were at a fine addition to the larder. The angler or shooter who came home empty-handed usually endeavoured to avoid meeting that excellent cook's eye, I noticed.

THE HADDIES OF THULE

Ten minutes after our home-coming there was 'a sound of frizzling by night,' and half an hour later ten persons might have been heard declaring that there were no haddocks in the whole wide world so good as those coming from Broad Bay, and no cook more admirable than Katie.

CHAPTER III

WILD DOGS AND TAME GROUSE

THE sport afforded by grouse in the Lews may be summed up in four words. Easy shooting, exhausting walking. Dogs are absolutely necessary, and we have a kennel full of beauties.

To-day there is an unwonted stir among the residents in the whitewashed little buildings at the back of the stables. Do they know, I wonder, that the first of September has arrived? That wise old retriever must have remembered that the coat Donald had on when he came with the biscuits was the very one he wears when out with the 'shentlemens,' and has communicated the fact to the rest. Even before breakfast there

WILD DOGS AND TAME GROUSE

are excited barkings, and glimpses of reddish-brown above the whitewash, as the Irish setters

'WE PAY AN EARLY VISIT TO THE KENNELS.'

leap up and endeavour to discover what is going on in the outer world beyond that low roughcast wall.

We pay an early visit to the kennels, and there is a general rush to the close-barred gate. Pat, the Irishman, panting, and with soft red tongue hanging out, eagerly greets us, sided by Spot, the Laverack, who looks up with gentle, appealing eyes.

An hour later we are on the moor.

There are five of us—two to shoot; Donald, the keeper, with a brace of dogs; Black Murdo to carry the game; and Long Murdo to lead the couple of Laverack setters, and bear on his broad shoulders the creel containing lunch.

We are crossing the snipe-bog near the sea, but our business is not with snipe to-day, and the dogs are not uncoupled until we reach higher, but not much drier ground, on which there is a poor apology for heather. On one side of us is the great bay dotted with the little craft from

WILD DOGS AND TAME GROUSE

which the thrifty crofters catch those excellent haddocks. Hawking for fish are great solan geese, which every few minutes make terrific dives through the air and send up a small waterspout as they disappear in the sea, bouncing up again in a second or two with a wriggling sand-eel in their beak. Sage-looking cormorants, sitting on a reef of rocks, flop heavily across the bay when my companion fires at a snipe which rises almost at his feet. Large gulls soar high in the air mysteriously, for though their wings move not, they seem to make headway against the wind. Small companies of blue rock-pigeons flit along by the cliffs; divers of many kinds bespeck the heaving water; of visible birds there is great plenty; but, though there is no cover worthy the name, and we have walked a mile over the moor, we have not seen a grouse.

It is a curious country this for grouse, or perhaps I should say that the grouse are oddly behaved. A man may walk over twenty miles of moorland well-stocked with birds, and yet not see more than two or three. Even with the best of dogs they are often most difficult to find, the scent on most days being anything but good. Before lunch it is nearly always bad, and I have known out of a bag of ten brace only one brace to be shot before two o'clock.

'Hold up,' says Donald the keeper, and two handsome red setters bound away over the moor. They are brother and sister these two, but as unlike each other, except as to size and colour, as two dogs can well be. Pat, the dog, is a gay, dashing fellow, with good-humoured laughing face, whose temper is absolutely perfect. Very much too gay and dashing is he to-day, for in the exuberance of his spirits he promptly springs a snipe, gives chase, marks it down, springs it again, gives chase again, marks it again, and repeats the performance until the snipe, unused to such conduct on the part of dogs, makes a long flight, and disappears over

WILD DOGS AND TAME GROUSE

the horizon, Pat in full chase. Just before we lose sight of him he dashes through a large

'A PIOUS OLD WOMAN.'

covey of grouse, which he disperses on all sides. At racehorse speed he rushes wildly on with gleaming teeth and red tongue hanging out. A pious old woman, who, clad in long black shawl, *boots*, and quaint headdress, is making her way across the moor to some religious meeting at the kirk, exhibits much consternation as the fierce-looking thing charges past her.

Not a very good beginning this to a day's shooting, nor one of those incidents which tend to make one shoot straight. Donald whistles vigorously without avail, and when he sees the grouse get up, says uncomplimentary things of Pat in Gaelic.

Meanwhile, Nelly, the bitch, apparently oblivious of the conduct of her bad brother, has been working slowly but very surely, and drawn on a snipe, over which she is patiently standing, looking round at us occasionally, as if to say—

'Why trouble yourselves about that silly fellow? Come and shoot what I have found for you.'

I say she is 'standing over' the snipe advisedly, for her one fault is getting too close to her birds. Early in the season that did not matter much, as both snipe and grouse lay like stones, and before the end of it she had found out the impropriety of her conduct. As I come up to her, leaving Donald to go after Pat, she turns a careworn, anxious face towards me, which plainly expresses the anxiety she feels lest the snipe should fly before I get within gunshot.

This dog is, as I said, the exact opposite of Pat. He is as fast and careless as she is slow and sure. He has a low-comedy face, which literally smiles all over. She has a high-bred, refined, delicate, anxious look, as if she regarded life as a very serious matter indeed. He is invariably good-tempered; she is uncertain and snappish, if annoyed or teased. There she stands, carefully watching a snipe, which I can see almost under her nose; and the snipe watches both of us wonderingly and in fear, but is so evidently a baby of a second brood, that I get Nelly to leave it, much to her disgust, and for a few minutes she refuses to work. She has to be coaxed and humoured into a good temper, and, after a few minutes, finds us two grouse, which we kill between us.

Donald comes up about this time leading Pat, who does not show in the slightest degree that he has any sense of his iniquity. Clearly, he is a dog without a conscience, and not of a high order of intelligence. He has to be punished, and with 'war chase' ringing in his ears he goes off on three legs, one being tucked under his collar. Even now, after he becomes accustomed to the loss of a leg, he ranges too wide for us, and indulges in an occasional chase; but at first he resents this treatment, by suddenly dropping several times as if to birds, deceiving even Donald himself, who says much in Gaelic. Our cup brims over when Nelly gets demoralised by her wicked brother; and runs in on a covey of grouse at which we do not get a shot.

WILD DOGS AND TAME GROUSE

Choleric men would probably have tried the effect of a charge of shot into Pat, but it is only his second season, and the early part of that; so much forbearance is shown, and after a while the order is given to couple him up. A day or two later Donald takes him carefully in hand, with the result that before the end of the year he is the best among the really good dogs in the kennel.

In the Outer Hebrides a wide ranging, strong dog is essential, as the birds are scattered and lie very close. Wide ranging and strong Pat certainly is, and when, later, under Donald's careful tuition, he becomes staunch and steady, he is the very dog for the work.

A grassy mound, the site of a deported crofter's hut, affords us a dry place for lunch, and we rest for half an hour and watch the solan geese feeding, and the porpoises tumbling in the bay. The dogs squat on their haunches at a respectful distance, and note with interest every particle of food which enters our mouths. A fragment is thrown to Nelly, who, seeing Pat glancing out of the corner of his eye at her, shows her teeth.

About two o'clock the two Laveracks are uncoupled, and begin to work beautifully. They were broken by Donald, and obey the slightest sign from him. Spot and Dot are their names. One takes the country for almost a quarter of a mile to the right of us, the other ranges as far to the left.

Suddenly Dot drops like a stone.

'Grouse,' says Donald laconically, and we walk towards the dog, who looks round to see if we are coming, but does not move a limb until Donald signs to him to approach the birds. Meanwhile the grouse have threaded their way between the peat hags, and Dot leads us after them with great care, though his body is quivering with excitement. Donald points to the droppings on the ground and whispers—

'A large covey.'

Dot now stops and will not budge an inch,

WILD DOGS AND TAME GROUSE

and, looking down, we see a lovely, bright-eyed grouse, squatting by the side of a small clump of heather, from which it is hardly distinguishable. But a bird on our right gets up first and falls to Gerald, my companion. His shot not only puts up the bird in front of us, but the rest of the covey, two of which we get.

Still, Dot does not stir, and not until we have reloaded and the game has been picked up does Donald say, 'Hold up.' But even then Dot, who knows his business, does not scamper off, but carefully works the ground near at hand, with the result that he finds a close-lying bird, which Gerald shoots.

'Did you see Spot?' asks Donald. 'She must have found birds, or she would have come up to us. She always backs Dot.' She is not to be seen, and Donald, telling us to watch Dot, goes after her. As soon as he is on a slightly higher ground he sees the bitch, holds up his hand, and we hear him cry to steady her. We join him, and there is Spot drawing on to game of some kind two hundred yards or so to the left of us.

'Ho!' cries Donald. 'Have a care, Spot,' and the bitch hears his voice and stands steady. We hurry over what Mr. Briggs would have called 'rather difficult country,' and as we get up to the bitch, an old cock-grouse appears on the top of a clump of heather and starts running.

'He is drawing the covey away,' says Donald, and presently he gets up, nearly out of gunshot, with a twist like a snipe. But it is his last twist in this world, for he tumbles with a broken wing. A small and very scattered covey get up and we kill two more.

It would be tedious to relate how we shoot a bird here and another there; but there are two incidents this afternoon which are worth recording. We are walking towards home, and are forced for a time to work the dogs down-wind. Dot, who is quartering the ground magnificently, suddenly, before he can stop, finds himself in the very middle

WILD DOGS AND TAME GROUSE

of a large covey. Nine out of ten dogs would lose their heads under the circumstances, but he simply drops at once and remains motionless. Five birds get up, but, seeing nothing to alarm them, settle again not more than twenty yards off. The rest of the covey does not stir. Two or three birds are right in front of the dog, and some on each side of him. But there he lies, and enables us to get a right and left at the birds close to him, and also to secure three of those which he had flushed. Those that escape then we follow up, and eventually shoot most of the covey.

A half-hour later Spot finds a solitary grouse, and stands steadily until we come up. We can see the bird—which is very tame—lying among the short heather about three yards in front of the bitch. It does not get up, and it seems as if the scent suddenly fails, for Spot leaves her point and takes a turn down-wind, apparently thinking the bird has escaped her. Donald is about to throw his whip at the bird to put it up, but we stop him, being curious to see what the bitch would do; but though she works towards us several times, and comes within a few yards of the grouse, she fails to get scent of it and eventually Donald kicks it up. It is certainly not a case of the bitch thinking she has done her duty when she has found the bird, and leaving us to do ours, for it is evident that she lost the bird and was eagerly looking for it, working the ground over and over again. As a rule she will never go twice over the same ground, and so finds more birds in a day than the other dogs.

I forget how many grouse we kill altogether, but it is a fair bag, and includes two blue hares, a rabbit, and some snipe. Though it is in September, the birds are still small. In fact, they are not shot at all on that moor until September 1, being little larger than thrushes on the Twelfth of August. All through the season we shoot them over dogs, and very delightful shooting it is, but towards Christmas they get a little wild.

CHAPTER IV

CONJURING SALMON

THE Gheira river flows out of a small loch some ten miles from the sea, cuts a very deep, narrow channel through the thick peat, forming at every bend a small pool, where salmon lie late in the season. Then, gaining volume by the addition of many tributary burns, it spreads somewhat, rippling over a rocky bed, until it comes within sight of the Bay, when, leaving the higher moors, it descends through a narrow gorge by a series of leaps—resting between each in a swirling pool—and finally calms down, as it winds through the flat alluvial lands below, and mingles its peat-stained waters with the billows of the Minch.

While awaiting spates, salmon and sea-trout collect in the tidal portions (or 'flats,' as they are called), the trutta giving very fair sport. Sometimes the salmon, on which it is said the crofters levy a heavy toll, rise to the fly, but that does not often happen on the flats. With the first July spate the fish push up into the series of rockbound pools caused by the somewhat abrupt descent of the river from the moor, and here they mostly stay until the middle or end of August, fresh fish joining them from time to time. Gradually a few begin to work higher up the stream, some, perhaps, even reaching the loch.

By degrees the pools in the gorge become untenanted, the fish crowding into the highest and largest of the series, where the bulk of them wait until nature's promptings and a September spate send them rollicking up towards the spawning-grounds. Then it is that the narrow, deep runs between the high peat banks, three or four miles below the loch, become well stocked with salmon, and, given a good rough wind to stir up the surface of these sheltered waters, the angler who ascends the river so far is often well rewarded.

An unusually fine take of salmon was made by Vernon, my host, from the largest pool of the lower or gorge series. The circumstances under which the fish were caught were remarkable. When the river was very low the stones at the bottom of the pool caused a break on the surface, and when very high, a strong stream swirled and eddied in pleasant fashion. But when the height of the water was neither high nor low the greater part of the pool was calm as any mill-pond.

The pool was at its calmest when Vernon made his big take. The atmosphere was dull and heavy, and the sky was hidden by leaden-coloured clouds. There was an air from the south-west, and a slight drizzle of rain fell almost unceasingly; but there was neither rain nor wind sufficient to ruffle the surface of the water. The pool was alive with fish. There was hardly a salmon to be found in the river below, and there was not sufficient water to carry the fish to the higher pools.

This was Vernon's first season with the salmon, but he had learned the importance of using fine tackle and small flies in calm water. He fished with a small Laxay at the end of a lake-trout cast, and very soon had a salmon take the fly under water. Others followed, and at the end of the day he had killed eight salmon of the usual Hebridean size, six of which were females.

Every fish took under water, and Vernon found that the best plan was to make no attempt to work the fly, but merely to cast it to the other side of the river and let the stream bring it round. The fish, for some reason or another, were undoubtedly taking in extraordinary fashion that day, not only in the Gheira but in other rivers in the island, as we afterwards heard. At the same time, Vernon owed much of his success to his delicate casting, for a lady who fished the same pool did not have a rise, though using the same fly and a fine cast. It was a most creditable performance for a man in his first season on a salmon river. A day or two later there came a series of spates, and the few remaining fish left their quarters for the higher pools.

My first visit to the upper reaches of the Gheira river was made too early in the season. There had been a series of spates, and the fish having had every opportunity of running up, Donald, the head-keeper, thought that a particular pool, named after one Joanna, a luckless crofter lass, might be worth a trial. Joanna, poor girl, when bearing a heavy creel of rushes on her back with which to mend the roof of her summer shieling, slipped into the river and was drowned. The fate of Joanna is remembered, but the name of the spot has been corrupted to 'Johnnie's pool.'

DAYS IN THULE

We, that is to say Miss Falconer, Frith, and myself, made an early start, and, by delaying not to fish on the way, arrived at the scene of Joanna's tragedy before eleven o'clock. Frith fished the pool, and hooked a large sea-trout which went off with the fly, thanks to a badly-tied knot. Miss Falconer whipped the river for brown trout, and I tried two pools below Johnnie's, named respectively the Major's and the White Bow pool.

Imagine if you can a sluggish stream of very dark, peat-stained water, about four feet in depth, some twelve feet in width, and perhaps a hundred and fifty yards in length. No ripple of any kind or sort, except when a gusty, shifty wind occasionally hit the surface of the water. About as unlikely a place for salmon as I ever saw, and not easy to fish. That was the Major's pool, which, to a certain major and other gallant anglers, had on occasions yielded as many as five salmon in a few hours.

Below this peculiar pool or, rather, miniature reach, the river took some very sharp S-shaped turns. It was there even narrower than the scene of the major's exploits, but, as I afterwards proved, a first-rate place for salmon, though terribly difficult to work properly, for the banks were high and fringed with flowering reeds, and one had to cast a long line to keep out of sight of the fish.

On that particular occasion the Major and the White Bow produced nothing. Frith having worked up the river, I tried Johnnie's pool, and rose a large fish twice, though the surface was calm as a plate-glass shop-window. He would not come a third time. After lunch, Donald took my rod for a few minutes and hooked a salmon, which broke away. But, if the salmon were not in the humour, the brown trout were most voracious. Frith and I each caught exactly thirty-three, running about four to the pound mostly, but including a few half-pounders.

These little fellows, which were all caught incidentally, seemed to think nothing of almost gorging a small Laxay.

Early in the afternoon we commenced to work homewards, fishing as we went, and hoping for kind fortune to favour us in the lower pools. About three o'clock Miss Falconer said she would like to try to catch a salmon, so I lent her my rod. We had just come to three small rocky pools, each a few feet above the one below. As Miss Falconer made her first cast into the centre pool there was a welcome swirl, but a too hurried strike disappointed both the fish and the angler. The fish was given a rest, and then rose again, but very short indeed. Miss Falconer was a little excited, and we had some difficulty to induce her to still further rest him. The third trial seemed likely to prove a failure, for a dozen or more casts were made without success, but suddenly the line tightened—the fish had seized the fly under water.

He was a lively fellow, and Miss Falconer, being

most anxious not to lose her first salmon, played him skilfully, but at the same time so delicately that he had a little too much his own way. However, after a visit to the pool above and another to the pool below, he returned to his starting-place, and showed signs of being about played out. But he was a wily fish, and just as Donald was approaching with the landing-net all motion suddenly ceased, the line remaining tight. There was a large stone, its top showing above the water some five feet from the bank, and under this the salmon had wriggled just like any eel.

We waited for five minutes or so, Miss Falconer anxiously holding the rod with line taut and ready to put on strain immediately the fish moved. Donald jumped on to the stone and poked about with his stick, with which he was able to touch the bottom. He opined that the fish was off and had left the fly fixed in a rock. Then I took his place, borrowed his stick, and felt gently down the line, tracing it to a small hole under the stone. Clearly the salmon had gone to earth like any fox, but it seemed not improbable that he had passed under the stone and out the other side, leaving the fly fixed. Just as I was coming to Donald's opinion, I felt a slight tremor on the line, and made up my mind that, after all, the fish was on.

We had no gaff with us, and I sighed for one of those little hooks with which congers and lobsters are inveigled out of holes on the Welsh coasts. But with us was a middle-aged man, one of the river-watchers, who had joined us on our way down, and he proved a very conjurer of fish—better than any gaff or conger-hook. A capital fellow was Kennie, but as a boy, so the story went, he was the terror of every gamekeeper in the district, and as much at home in the river as out of it. He commenced by being a fisherman-crofter, like most of the men in the island, but his boat was wrecked and he was all but drowned, so, having a wife and a family to

CONJURING SALMON

support, he was thankful when Donald very judiciously made him river-watcher. He was a

'DID I EFFER POACH A SAUMON?—OH, AY!'

merry little man, notwithstanding his misfortunes, with bright, twinkling black eyes, an intelligent face, and no English to speak of, which made conversation with him difficult.

I took Kennie's photo one day. It was no difficult matter to get him to look pleasant.

'Did you ever poach a salmon, Kennie?' I queried, as I pointed the Kodak at him.

'Did I effer poach a saumon?—oh, ay!—' and he stopped to consider the most judicious reply, or, perhaps, how to express himself in English. The camera meanwhile made its record.

As soon as I gave out that the salmon was still at the end of the line, Donald and Kennie confabulated in Gaelic. I was watching the line anxiously when Miss Falconer said suddenly, 'Oh, how very annoying!' put the rod into my hand, and beat a hasty retreat.

I was momentarily puzzled, but, looking round, saw that Kennie, who had retired a few yards away, had taken off his coat, and was unbuttoning his braces. I confess that I, too, misinterpreted these movements, but after various manœuvres with his nether garments which need not be described in detail, it came out that the man's only anxiety was for the dryness of his shirt-tails, which he tucked up under his waistcoat.

With clothing in decent order he and Donald walked into the water to attempt the overturning of the stone, and Miss Falconer was called back to hold the rod until the bitter end, which she was very anxious to do. But the end was not yet, for the stone refused to be moved. Donald next tried to get his stick under it, but that caused a further retreat of the fish into its stronghold by about six inches. Still, it was something to feel the fish move. Then Kennie put his arm under, but failed to touch the fish, and there seemed as if nothing more could be done.

We looked blankly at one another. Was it possible that four men and a woman could be beaten by a salmon well-hooked and lying under a stone within five feet of them? Should we, after all, be obliged to break the line and go home salmonless?

'If he canna get him, no one can,' said Donald, pointing to the watcher, who grinned at the compliment.

'Try once more, Kennie,' said I; 'you must have put your hand within an inch of the fish.'

'Oh, ay,' said Kennie, and finished his sentence in another tongue. He made one more determined effort, regardless of the dryness of his cherished shirt, suddenly exclaimed something in Gaelic, and jumped out on to the bank. 'He felt the fish,' explained Donald, and I fell a-wondering why, if he felt the fish, he should leave it in such a hurry. But Kennie knew what he was about, and there followed the smartest conjuring performance I had ever seen. Never did Herr Soandso or Professor Thingumi produce a pumpkin from an old gentleman's hat with greater dexterity than did Kennie—but I must not anticipate.

Quickly rolling up his blue serge trousers, he whipped off the piece of tanned cod-line which did duty for garter, and bent a running noose, which he slipped over his left wrist. Then he rushed into the river, and, with a glorious disregard of wet shirt, bent down until his face touched the water, and groped with both hands under the stone. A second or two later he suddenly hauled out the salmon by the cod-line, the noose round its tail, and flung it on the bank. Even then we nearly lost the fish, for the bank was sloping. But we all flung ourselves upon the unfortunate creature, and somehow or other worked it into the landing-net and carried it in triumph up on to the heather. And all this time the hook held.

Kennie, beaming, came up out of the water, and was warmly praised and rewarded; but when I asked him if he had ever landed a fish that way before he said nothing, but looked volumes.

The noose is often used by Hebridean fish-poachers. One end of the line they fasten to their waist, and with the noose over the left wrist, walk in and search under well-known and shelving-rocks for salmon. On feeling one they work the noose from their wrist over their hand, and gently insinuate it over his tail, then calmly walk out, sometimes in sight of a watcher on the hill-top, who does not see the fish dragged along the ground. Even if he does suspect anything the men are hidden in a gully among the peat bog in a second, and the ground is so broken that they can easily escape.

Miss Falconer was very proud of her salmon, and the little Blue Doctor with which it was caught forms the decorative part of a brooch, and is among her most cherished possessions.

CHAPTER V

DUCK, PLOVER, AND SNIPE

DUCK, teal, and widgeon were anything but plentiful on the moors shot over by the tenants of Gheira Lodge, and for this reason, perhaps (such is human nature), the greatest anxiety was exhibited by some of us to shoot them. Several long fruitless tramps to distant lochs were undertaken after phantom flocks of wildfowl, and the more enthusiastic among us hid in 'demned moist unpleasant' places about nightfall in hopes, which were invariably disappointed, of shooting the birds during their evening flight.

There was, however, one place where some very fair shooting might be had, but only lasting, at most, an hour. At the bottom of a deep valley lay two lochs, one round, the other an irregular oval. Originally they doubtless formed one sheet, but the level of the water fell, and at the time we made their acquaintance they were some fifty yards apart, a tiny brooklet trickling from one to the other through a grassy bank. The Lochs of the Mill (or its Gaelic equivalent) they were called, but not even the ruin of a mill remained. Containing extensive reed-beds, they were much frequented by duck and other wildfowl, which, when disturbed in one loch, had the amiable and praiseworthy habit of simply flying to the other, usually passing over the grassy bank above mentioned. This bank was not more than 20 yards in width. In the moor, which rose sharply on each side, deep gullies cut by the winter rains afforded splendid natural 'butts' for the wildfowler.

Quietly and cautiously we used to steal down between the peat hags and take up our positions by the side of the grassy bank. A gillie would then be sent to the reed-beds in one of the lochs to shout and disturb the birds. Some days the duck were in a restless humour and flew right away, but usually they showed a strange reluctance to leave the spot, and came flying rapidly towards the other loch, in which case one at least of us had an opportunity of emptying a couple of barrels. Even after we had fired, a few birds would occasionally alight in the reed-beds, and after a little while allow themselves to be driven back again. Certainly I never met more accommodating ducks.

In the Lews the chances of finding the birds on any particular loch depend in a great measure on the height of the water, which, in that land of sudden rainstorms, is apt to vary rapidly and considerably. The lower the water the more cover of course there is for the birds. Sometimes a loch might be so full that only a few inches of reeds showed above the surface, and there was practically no available cover. In lochs other than the two once utilised by the ancient Hebridean miller, the duck were not by any means accommodating, and it used to be a most difficult matter to get a shot at them. I am referring to the autumn: in hard weather they would of course be less shy.

When walking over the moor one day, rod in hand, testing a number of rarely-fished lochs, I happened upon a great flock of wild geese feeding on an islet in a loch, the shores of which were mostly composed of fragments of white quartz very different to anything else I had seen in the island. Another day a pair of great northern divers flew over our heads carrying fish from the sea to their young. The two most noteworthy birds I saw were a white eagle and a snow-bunting.

Golden plover were as plentiful as ducks, and other waterfowl were scarce, but I did not see a single lapwing. After the crops were cleared, great flocks of golden plover came down to feed

DUCK, PLOVER, AND SNIPE

on the crofts, and were usually to be found on the crofter's strips of land or on the meadows near the lodge. Failing these two places, they were probably feeding on the flats by the mouth of the river. These birds were often almost unapproachable, but occasionally they would let one walk straight up to, or rather a little to one side of them, and get within gunshot, particularly if they were feeding on the grass. This doubtless happened when they were fatigued after long flights.

We used to kill many plover by hiding behind stone walls or banks and waiting for them. If they did not see us when we fired, they would, as often as not, fly over our heads a second time, so it was well to reload quickly. During the season we shot a goodly number of these birds, but more would have been killed if the ploverists, to coin a new word, had gone out by themselves, and not in parties of three or four. It is difficult to arrange a golden-plover battue.

On the large tracts of land devoted to peat-cutting—black, unfertile, desolate-looking places, we rarely found game of any kind. Doubtless the birds were disturbed by the women and

'BLACK, UNFERTILE, DESOLATE-LOOKING PLACES.'

children who, after the peat cocks (if I may use the term) were dry, carried their invaluable and pleasant fuel to the stacks by their cabins.

DUCK, PLOVER, AND SNIPE

Perhaps, too, there was little food for wildfowl in such places.

Those most wily of feathered creatures, the curlews, were sometimes seen. I could have shot many of them when I was salmon-fishing had my rod been a gun. Whenever we were ready for them they kept well out of range. Wise birds! We did not shoot or even get a shot at one during our three months' sojourn on the moor, but we made no great efforts in that direction.

The tender, juicy snipe of Thule are a pleasant memory. The principal snipe bog was a strip of land a quarter of a mile wide, let us say, by about two miles in length. It stretched along the coast on the tops of the cliffs at a considerable height above sea-level. One hardly expects to find snipe bogs on cliff-tops, but there are many curious things in the Lewis. One great charm about that bog was its position so near the lodge. When there was no time to fish salmon or to go after grouse, or to launch the boat, one could always slip a few cartridges in one's pocket, let loose Nelly or Dot, and perhaps within ten minutes kill a snipe—possibly two. Indeed, the former tenant actually kicked one up and shot it as he was walking from the lodge to the kennel, a distance of forty yards.

Certainly it was an unfortunate thing for the snipe that they had made their quarters so near us. Most of them, I fancy, were home-bred birds, but there must have been not a few strangers as well, for however many we shot, their numbers never seemed to be any the less. Whatever day or whatever time we walked that bog the dogs were certain to find snipe for us. Of how many places in either England or Ireland can this be said?

First one would come upon a moist place, let us say, covered with rank grasses, rushes and moss, then the land would rise slightly and we would find ourselves on dry, heather-covered moorland. Then at the bottom of the slope there would be more soft places. Moorland and

DUCK, PLOVER, AND SNIPE

bog alternated quickly, and this was perhaps the reason why the snipe were always at home. In Ireland I have often noticed that some days the snipe are on the moors, on others in the bogs. Here the birds had both moist feeding-place and dry cover at hand, so became nice agreeable stay-at-home creatures, always ready when wanted.

While after snipe we often happened on grouse, blue hares, and rabbits. This increased the pleasure of shooting along the cliff-tops, though it rendered the question of the best-sized shot to be used a difficult one. Some of us swore by No. 6. I, contrary to the opinion of some shooters of experience, believed in having No. 8 in my right barrel and No. 6 in my left.

Right pleasant were the tramps over that moorland bog, particularly when the dogs worked well. They enabled me to thoroughly understand the enthusiasm of old-fashioned sportsmen over their setters and pointers. I am in full sympathy with them. To my mind the use of well-trained dogs to find the game doubles the pleasures of shooting. Unfortunately one has to go to a place about two centuries behind the rest of Great Britain to obtain an opportunity of working them.

CHAPTER VI

A SULKY SALMON AND A GREEDY COD

EARLY morning fishing does not find great favour with any considerable number of anglers, and is certainly in strong disfavour with the great majority of anglers' attendants. From the day, some twenty years ago, when a weather-beaten old Thames fisherman assured me that fish never bit in the rain, I have always had the classical grain of salt ready to swallow with any statements made by professional fishermen and gillies respecting those habits of fish which would be likely to lead to their own personal inconvenience.

Thus it was that, notwithstanding the solemn assurance that the fish in the Gheira river—

whatever they might do elsewhere—never rose before ten in the morning or after six in the evening, I turned out of bed early one glorious day in August last, and, after partaking of a crust of bread and some whisky and milk—the latter doled out by an unwilling' dairymaid, who objected muchly to disturbing the night's cream —I took my favourite split-cane rod from the long box outside the lodge, and hied me to the waterside.

Though the morning was glorious in one sense —glorious with brilliant sunlight,—it was anything but suitable for salmon-fishing, for there was absolutely no wind. Yet one had not the heart to complain. Crossing the meadows intervening between the lodge and the open moor were the cows on their way to be milked. Dewdrops sparkled on each blade of grass, larks flew up at almost every footstep, and just on the edge of the moor a snipe suddenly rose almost at my feet and whizzed away over the valley. Close

A SULKY SALMON AND A GREEDY COD

to their homes in the old, unmortared stone walls, rabbits were nibbling the tender grass-shoots, oblivious of the fate they were to meet on the morrow, through the instrumentality of certain newly-purchased ferrets.

Twenty yards distant, on the top of a heathery knoll, a fine-looking old cock grouse boldly showed himself, with the object, doubtless, of calling away my attention from his youngsters, which were crouching in the low covert around him. Hovering in the air were two immense blackback gulls, birds which have the reputation, by the way, of being arrant poachers. I never saw them destroy anything worthy of preservation, but that proves nothing.

The river was low, but it held fish—sulky fish, for was it not August? A walk of a mile brought me sufficiently far from the lodge to commence fishing, but the first pool was too like a looking-glass to be cast over. As I neared the bank gentle swells in the water (some one looking over my shoulder says this is suggestive of mashers bathing, but anglers well know the sign) going, some in one direction, some another, evidenced the fact that there were salmon in the pool, and that they had seen the angler on the bank. The cast was clearly no use, so I hurried down the river, trying the heads of various pools, where the in-running water gave one some chance of putting a fly over a fish without scaring him.

Here and there a fish leaped out of the water; but for nearly two hours none rose at the fly. I had reached the lowest salmon-holding pool on the river, and it wanted five minutes of breakfast-time. That feeling of being superior to one's fellow-men which all early risers feel (provided their early rise is unwonted) had departed, and hopelessness had taken its place.

'One cast more for luck, and then home,' said I to Kennie, who had joined me.

The fly went out across to the opposite bank and swung slowly round behind a huge

A SULKY SALMON AND A GREEDY COD

boulder, rising from the bank on my side of the river, where it was lost to sight. Then suddenly came a great pull and a splash, the reel gave out that music most pleasant to the angler's ear, and I was firm in a fish, how large or how small could not be said.

Verily the situation was not by any means a pleasant one, for the mass of rock projected into the river, and I was on one side of it and the fish on the other. Fortunately the line, which was rubbing on the boulder, met no sharp edge, and in a few seconds I was able to scramble over the top of the obstruction, by which time the fish had gone half-way down the pool. After cruising about there awhile, he swam rapidly up to the head again, into the fast-running water, whence I moved him as soon as possible, fearing the line would be cut on the sharp edges of some shelving rock.

Cunningly he next sought refuge almost under my feet, near the tail of the pool, where the peat bank overhung, and was lined here and there with a short scrubby growth. As he left this place of danger—that is, dangerous from my point of view—he came close to the surface, and proved to be no monster, but a salmon of no extraordinary dimensions. But though not large, he made up for lack of weight in strength, endurance, and cunning, and tried every dodge known to salmon to get free. Jiggering was the least of them, and, as when that happens fish are very often but lightly hooked, I was afraid to put a very heavy strain on him. Once only he leapt, and, finding it was a waste of strength, made no further attempt in that direction.

A shepherd with two friendly collie dogs came and looked on. Shortly afterwards there appeared on the opposite bank another watcher, called Long Kenneth, to distinguish him from the merry little gillie. He sat on the bank complacently smoking, now and again exchanging a word or two of Gaelic with Kennie, who had

'HE SAT ON THE BANK COMPLACENTLY SMOKING.'

not much English. It was then about half-past nine, and the fish, though it had been hooked half an hour, showed no signs of giving in, but, perhaps feeling he required a rest, retired to the deepest part of the pool and sulked.

Stoning was of no avail; but at ten o'clock, the fish having been on an hour, I screwed up some paper into a ring, passed it over the rod and down the line, whence it was carried by the stream over his nose. The paper he objected to, so made a run the length of the pool, jiggered a little, freed himself of the encumbrance, and retired to his lair to sulk as before.

At half-past ten, along a winding path came a little army bearing rods — two ladies, two knights, and four esquires; or, in prosaic nineteenth century language, male and female anglers, a keeper, and gillies. To these I sent Kennie to beg for food and whisky, and they (the animate ones, not the comestibles) all trooped down to see the performance.

A SULKY SALMON AND A GREEDY COD

After five minutes the ladies expressed their opinion that the delights of playing salmon had been grossly exaggerated by anglers, as all they saw to amuse them was a weary and hungry individual sitting on the bank with his line apparently fastened to the bottom of the river. However, another ring of paper created a 'divarsion,' as Pat says.

In some ways a good sulk on the part of a fish is not an unmixed evil. It gives rest to the arms, and in this case allowed a famished mortal to partake of whisky and sandwiches with some degree of comfort. In the words of the programme, there was 'an interval for refreshments.'

On the curtain being raised, further travellers were sent down the line to the fish, who, also much refreshed, renewed some of his old tactics. I begged the onlookers to go fishing, and not waste their valuable time watching so poor a performance; but no, they would see the end on 't.

Everything, except eternity and new fashions

in ladies' dress, has an end; but it was not until half-past eleven, some two hours and a half after he was hooked, that this fish gave in. To the last he fought gamely. The keeper had the gaff, but Kennie, eager to land a fish which he had seen hooked and played, possessed himself of a landing-net, and twice got the salmon halfway in it, only to let him fall out again into the water.

I dare not write what I said to Kennie, but I had to say it several times (he having, as I have said, but little English) before he would put down the net, with which he was far less handy than with the noose or gaff. Then Donald stooped down, and a second later a shapely cock fish, of no great size, lay on the grass. Usually small salmon take, at the outside, a quarter of an hour to kill on light tackle; but this fish had extraordinary staying powers. It was very lightly hooked by a little piece of skin on the edge of the lower jaw, and would have unques-

A SULKY SALMON AND A GREEDY COD

tionably been lost if I had not played him lightly. A lot of pother about a small fish, some may say; but though small, the creature was a Samson among salmon.

After a rest and a further incursion into the luncheon basket, I joined the ladies, who had left as soon as the fish was landed, and, after vainly endeavouring to get a salmon on to their lines, returned with them to the lodge.

In the afternoon it was suggested that the fishing-boat should be launched, and four of us, with a crew of two, sailed out over the sparkling and lively waters of the bay, lively because at sea there was a breeze which we had not felt on the river. About two miles or so from land we anchored, and, while the others fished with hand-lines, I used a single salmon-gut paternoster, fitted with eyed hooks, a Nottingham reel and line, and a pike rod.

The haddies bit freely, and as the lug-worms were running short, I began baiting with pieces of haddock. Presently there came a dead weight and steady strain on the pike rod, and line commenced to run out slowly. Twenty yards went off the reel. Then the fish stopped an instant, but soon went on steadily and irresistibly. I suggested cod, and feared halibut. Long Murdo rather thought it was a big dog-fish, but Black Murdo and I doubted this, as dog-fish are more lively than was the one being played. For full twenty minutes he swam slowly about the bottom, then suddenly gave up the ghost, and came to the surface, with much-inflated belly upwards, some distance from the boat. It was a large cod —too large for our landing-net.

The fish ceased biting, so we weighed anchor, and soon made our landing-place. Of haddies there were forty-four, all in most excellent condition, weighing over $\frac{1}{2}$ cwt., while the cod weighed $12\frac{1}{2}$ lb. Inside him was a haddock, and in the haddock a hook, fastened to a piece of hair snooding. The cod had evidently swal-

A SULKY SALMON AND A GREEDY COD
lowed a haddock which had been hooked on some long lines set by crofters near our boat, and had then broken off the snooding, and, in search of further adventures, came across my paternoster, and been caught as related.

CHAPTER VII

AN ASSAULT ON THE BLUE ROCK STRONGHOLDS

 CERTAIN Eastern gentleman once described in *The Field* the sport of dove-shooting, as carried on in the neighbourhood of Alexandria. If I remember aright, a tree on which doves were in the habit of resting in their flight was the chief essential; under its spreading branches the gunner took his stand, and potted the birds as they alighted. Not a very high form of sport, perhaps, but one in which it would not be difficult to become proficient in a short space of time, and possessing the merit of not conducing to fatigue on the part of the sportsman.

Probably almost every Englishman who possesses a gun has attempted something of the kind on our own shy and almost shot-proof wood-pigeons, but comparatively few persons have had the privilege—for I call it nothing else—of shooting the wild blue rocks in their haunts on the rugged coasts of the North of England, Ireland, Scotland, and the Hebrides.

Putting aside those forms of sport in which there is considerable danger, there is no shooting more exciting or more difficult than that which is afforded by these fast-flying and thickly-feathered little birds. A man who is fairly certain of four out of five snipe will probably find himself at first killing only one or two pigeons out of ten shots, sometimes not even so many.

The birds fly through the air with extraordinary rapidity, and, as they usually dart out of the caves from six to twenty at a time, it is most difficult to single out a bird. It is rare that a shot into the 'brown'—if such may be said of 'blue rocks'—produces anything more than smoke and noise. Speaking from my own experience, I should say that nothing is more likely to improve a man's shooting than a week or so devoted to the wild rock-pigeons. The gun must be brought smartly to the shoulder, and must be pointed well ahead of the birds; and any one who has acquired the habit of taking what I may call a rifle aim will speedily find himself cured. From fifteen to twenty-five yards is about the best distance at which to take these birds, for, if they are allowed to go much further, the shot has little effect on them, unless a stray pellet chances to hit them on a particularly vulnerable part.

The days we spent cruising along the coast to the northward of Broad Bay I shall long remember as being amongst the most enjoyable of any we devoted to shooting. Once, when half a gale from the west was blowing, it was arranged that while most of our party should drive to a very lovely bay some seven miles distant, and there pass the day shooting rabbits on the rocky sides of the cliffs, or ferreting them out of their burrows in the sand-hills, three of us should work our way down the coast, shooting pigeons on the way, and join the others in the evening. We three consisted of Miss Falconer, who loved nothing better than to handle the tiller on these expeditions, especially when a little sea-fishing was part of the programme; Talbot, a first-rate shot, good sailor, and capital companion; and the writer.

We were rather late in starting, and the men, though they uttered not a word, were evidently reluctant to go any distance from home on such a wild morning. There was no alacrity shown in getting the boat launched, and it was almost noon before we were fairly under weigh. With two reefs in our lug-sail, we bowled through the water seven or eight miles an hour, but our speed fell off when, having sailed out of the sheltered nook where some herring-boats lay at anchor, we changed our course from east to north, and were sheltered from the strong west wind by the cliffs.

DAYS IN THULE

Passing several caves which were not in high favour with the pigeons, we stopped first at two considerable caverns, lofty enough for our boat, mast and all, to enter for some little distance.

'THE SHELTERED NOOK WHERE SOME HERRING-BOATS LAY AT ANCHOR.'

A shout from the men, and a solitary pigeon flew out, at which neither of us fired, expecting others to follow. But, with that exception, these caves were devoid of birds, or, I should say, pigeons, for a cloud of starlings flew out with a great fluster which caused our guns to go up involuntarily to our shoulders.

Further northward was an immense cavity in the conglomerate known as the Pigeon Cave. In former times it was, no doubt, worthy its name, but now, owing probably to its being very accessible from the shore, it rarely contains many birds. Here we landed and took our places on the slippery rocks, while one of the men went into the cave. Only two pigeons flew out, and neither of these we killed, though both were feathered. As a matter of fact, it was as yet a little too early to find the pigeons at home, most of them being away feeding. Hearing our shots, the gillie brought the boat round the corner to pick up the dead birds, and picked us up instead.

We had next to sail across an open bay, and were exposed to the full force of the wind, which came sweeping down a broad valley; but in about ten minutes we had reached across, and were under shelter of the cliffs, which here were lofty, and very rugged and broken. Within a few hundred yards were not less than a dozen caves, and many fissures and crevices in the rocks, nearly all of which contained pigeons. At this spot we commenced to have some really good shooting.

The mast and sail having been lowered, we rowed behind a small rocky islet, on which were hundreds of cormorants and other sea-birds, and turned into a small bay, at the end of which was a great cleft in the rocks, commencing below low-water mark and reaching up some forty feet or more. It was a shallow cave, and had to be approached very quietly. As we drew near, two pigeons saw us, and flew out, but did not come within range. Approaching the rocks as closely as we dared, for the swell was considerable, I made the men steady the boat and then shout. A cloud of pigeons darted out. Talbot and I both had a right and left. Two birds fell dead into the water, another was very hard hit, and we picked him up a little further along the coast. A fourth bird shed enough feathers to stuff a pillow (more or less), but beyond effecting this unnatural moult seemed none the worse for our attentions.

It is very important, when shooting blue rocks, to get all way on the boat stopped before any noise is made, and it should be the particular care of the men to keep the boat in position, and not let it be carried on by wind or tide. The rowers should not be gaping round to see the pigeons fly out, but should give their whole attention to the boat. If there is any way on, the shooter has an additional and unnecessary motion to contend with. The pigeons are moving either to the right or left, the boat rises and falls with the swell, and if you add to these motions an unnecessary forward movement, the chances are very much in favour of the pigeons. While on the practical portion of the subject, I would advise those who shoot blue rocks for the first time to enforce upon the boatmen the importance of not shouting until they are told to do so. The order should not be given until the boat is steady and properly placed, and both guns are ready, with a couple of extra cartridges at hand to go into the chambers immediately after firing. It sometimes happens that a second or two after the first flight of birds one or more pigeons will fly out, and this very often occurs when the guns are not ready for action.

With regard to the best size of shot, I found No. 5 answer very well, particularly if I did not let the birds go too far, and at short ranges No. 6 compassed the death of a good many birds. No doubt larger shot (No. 2 or 3) would kill at longer ranges if a pellet or two struck the bird, but larger shot means fewer shot, and a pigeon forty yards distant may easily be in the direct line of fire, and yet be untouched by a single pellet. But I believe I am correct in saying that if large shot be used, the birds are either

ASSAULT ON BLUE ROCK STRONGHOLDS

altogether missed or brought down; if No. 5 or No. 6 be preferred, the great point is to attempt no long shots.

During the day I went on shore and found a place where a photograph of the boat could be taken. Indeed, fortune favoured me so much that I was able to open the lens at the very moment one of those who were on board fired, and the smoke from the gun is plainly visible. As a rule we had no sail up when shooting, but some ladies had come on board, and had been enjoying a short cruise along the coast.

Leaving the bay, we rowed along until we came to three very remarkable caves side by side, not a half-dozen yards dividing them. They were deep, and no pigeons were visible, but on a ledge of rock sat three solemn-looking cormorants. In which cave were the pigeons? If we took the first, the birds might fly out of the third one, and *vice versâ*. Finally, we decided to place the boat at the mouth of the centre one, and take the

'I WAS ABLE TO OPEN THE LENS AT THE VERY MOMENT ONE OF THOSE WHO WERE ON BOARD FIRED.'

chance of any birds there were in the side caves flying out within gunshot. In this we were unfortunate. The shouts of the men produced nothing, so our fair helmswoman fired a shot into the cave from a rook-rifle we had brought with us for the purpose. The sound of the shot went echoing into the bowels of the earth, and a second later four or five pigeons were seen flying swiftly out of the darkness towards us. Thinking that we should very likely fire at the same birds, I left these for Talbot, who shot one of them.

As bad luck would have it, there was not a bird in the cave on my side, while from the one on the right flew forty or fifty pigeons, which went away without a shot being fired at them, Talbot having emptied both barrels at the birds which came out of the centre cave. However, there was not much to grieve over, for the pigeons were certain to seek refuge in one of their haunts further northward, and the probability was that we should come across them before the day was over.

About this time, the wind having much increased, we had some doubts as to the prudence of joining the rabbit-shooters, who were working the cliffs about two miles distant. We finally decided to keep our appointment, and at the same time avoid any unnecessary danger by landing on the southern side of a certain wave-beaten point, and attain our destination by a walk of a mile or so.

It would take too much space to describe all the incidents of that day, and the wonders and beauties of that rocky and cavernous coast, which is one of the most remarkable in Great Britain.

At one spot a great wall of rock reared itself a hundred feet or more above our heads, and at right angles to the line of coast. For some unexplainable reason the wind here changed its direction, and blew right off the face of the rock and against the swell which was breaking on it. As a result, the sea seemed to boil, and, though there was no real danger, the situation was not one which a nervous person would have enjoyed. A miniature waterfall, the result of some heavy showers, was pouring down from the top of the cliff, but before it reached the sea the wind caught it up and whirled it hither and thither, letting it fall somewhere or other, I suppose, in the form of fine spray. There was also a good deal of salt-water in the air.

At the foot of the great rock was a deep cave with a low entrance, into which we had seen several pigeons fly. But it was a difficult place to get at, as, leaving the wild wind and seething sea out of consideration, a rock, about as great as a crofter's cottage, rose out of the water immediately in front of the cave, and on this the sea was breaking. Even when we did get within gunshot of the place, it was next to impossible to keep the boat in position for an instant, the wind was so strong. After two failures the men managed to hold the boat for a few seconds, during which the rifle was fired to frighten the birds. Only one pigeon flew out at first, but Talbot shot it, and the noise of his gun brought out the rest, and I managed to bring one down.

A little further and we came upon a coal-black, bleating lamb perched on a ledge of rock about 20 feet above high-water mark. How it got down there was a mystery; but one thing was clear, without assistance it could never get up again, nor anywhere but into the sea. It was a nasty place at which to land, owing to the swell, and the rock coming down almost sheer into the water, but the attempt was made, and one of us got the lamb under his arm, and without accident brought it safely into the boat. It was very light, so had probably been some days in its unpleasant position. Still higher up the cliff were a ewe and a lamb, both horned and well-bred little Highland sheep. They were in as great a fix as the lamb we had rescued, but we could do nothing for them from below. A day later they were rescued from above by means of ropes.

Shortly after taking the coloured passenger on board we rounded a bold headland, and were confronted by a magnificent natural monolith rising up out of the sea, majestic and grand. At some past age it was probably connected with the cliffs. Now it stands like a giant sentinel on that ironbound coast.

As we rested on our oars, admiring this splendid freak of nature, a small flock of pigeons came flying swiftly along the face of the cliffs. Being behind the pillar of rock, we were hidden from them, and they suddenly appeared within easy gunshot. T.'s gun was up to his shoulder in an instant, mine followed, and a second later two birds lay on their backs in the water. The pigeons were flying so fast that there was literally no time to get a second shot. The birds we had killed having been retrieved by means of a landing-net—which, by the way, we found most useful,—we tried two or three more blue-rock strongholds, and then, rounding a ledge of rocks which projected some distance into the sea, we came within sight of our landing-place, called in Gaelic, Port Mohr, the said 'big port' consisting of a stretch of white sand at the foot of the cliffs.

I thought of that ancient conundrum about a 'heavy swell pitching into a little cove' on the island which Robinson Crusoe would otherwise have considered to be uninhabited, the conditions were so exactly similar. We ran our boat ashore on the sand, some fisher lads, who had been watching us from the cliff-top, coming down and rendering valuable assistance. But while the little cove received us with open arms, the heavy swell showed a distinct lack of good-breeding by boarding us over the stern and covering our helmswoman with water.

The little black lamb now led the way up the cliffs, and the boat having, with much labour,

ASSAULT ON BLUE ROCK STRONGHOLDS

been dragged above high-water mark, we followed up the water-worn precipitous path, and half an hour later fell in with the rabbit-shooting party. They, we found, had lost their ferrets, and spent the day vainly endeavouring to lure down by means of decoys the blue-rocks flying between the cliffs and the crofts, where the grain crops were ripening, a method which is occasionally very successful.

CHAPTER VIII

THREE LOCHS AND A PUDDLE

FRESH from fishing a trout stream, where every fish was an old acquaintance, each pebble a landmark, and where I knew almost the blades of grass by the river-side, great indeed was the enjoyment of coming to this land of lochs, where on each of a hundred days there was fresh water to be whipped, where trout existed in millions, where the dry fly was unknown and unneeded, and where fish were counted by the dozen rather than by the brace. It was a land of enchantment for the trout-fisher. There were lochs never yet struck by the angler's flies. There were lochs where the fish averaged nine

THREE LOCHS AND A PUDDLE

to the pound, and yet within a few paces were other waters where the fishermen might catch goodly pounders which fought like demons. Then one might fish for other trout as large as the aforesaid demons, but which did not fight at all. There were lochs with white-fleshed trout, lochs with pink-fleshed trout, lochs with yellow-fleshed trout.

The variety offered was bewildering and unsettling. If the fish were taking but badly in Loch Bacabhat, away we were apt to run to Loch an Eoira, not two hundred yards distant, where the trout ran smaller, but rose freer. Returning in the evening we would doubtless find that those who had stayed and persevered at Bacabhat had been rewarded, whilst we had only fingerlings to show for our pains.

With so many good things to choose from, it will be understood that we were not so active as we might have been in trying the uncertain lochs, those which were not usually fished by the tenants of Gheira Lodge. Thus it happened that September had arrived before we decided to try a loch some three miles distant, which the head-keeper said no one in living memory had ever fished, but which he knew held trout, as once, when resting by its banks after a long tramp over the moor, he saw several good fish rising. Donald, a sportsman to the backbone, was as keen after trout and salmon as he was after grouse, and on that September morning, when we started for Loch an Fheoir Ghrinnabhat, confessed he would rather have been with us than looking after the grouse-shooters. Long Murdo, who went with us, did not know the way, but he was given many directions by Donald, and we took with us a good map and a compass, without which I doubt if we should have found the loch.

I am glad to be able to give a portrait of our most worthy Murdo. He was an excellent gillie, though somewhat lacking in cheerfulness, the result of having faced death one winter's night in the Minch, when the boat he was on

'THE ONE OCCASION ON WHICH I MADE HIM LAUGH OUTRIGHT.'

foundered. However, he looks sufficiently cheerful in the photograph. I believe this was the one occasion on which I made him laugh outright. I would I also had a portrait of Donald, the keeper, who told me of the loch I am writing about. Unfortunately all my 'shots' at him failed.

This loch of the Grassy Banks, to give it its English name, lay high among the hills. First we trudged up a green valley, down which trickled a little stream. Snipe rose now and again at our feet, and curlew flew whistling over our heads. Soon we came to an ancient turf-wall, which may have divided the territories of some ancient Hebridean chieftains. The top of it now forms a useful path for anglers going to the loch.

Up, up we went, and suddenly found ourselves enveloped in mist. This was awkward, for the saddle between the twin tops of a certain distant mountain had been our mark. Fortun-

THREE LOCHS AND A PUDDLE

ately we had the compass, and taking our bearings very carefully, we went on and soon struck the lower end of a considerable piece of water known as Loch Langabhat. A little higher and we found ourselves above the mist and in sight of three lochs. These Murdo was able to name, and, thus finding out our exact position by means of the map, we slightly altered our direction, and in about half an hour reached the mysterious loch where living man had never yet cast a fly. At least Donald said so, and I have no reason to think he was mistaken. It was a small loch, perhaps not more than a hundred yards in length, lying in a hollow on the top of the moor. The water was black even for the Hebrides, and appeared very deep. We reached it on the sheltered side and parted, Westbury, my companion, going round to the right, I working to the left.

Knowing that trout, when little fished for, are partial to large flies, I put up a small salmon fly—a fiery brown, which had answered well on other occasions, and an ordinary lake-trout fly as a dropper.

Not a rise was to be seen. By the bank on my side the water was absolutely calm, but by making a long cast I could just reach out to the commencement of the ripple. For some time I toiled vainly, casting out as far as possible. Drawing my fly in close to the bank, a large fish of at least 2 lb. swam out and seized it, which so astonished me that I failed to strike and merely ejaculated. That was weak, no doubt, but we all do weak things at times. This incident led to my fishing the water close to the banks, and there, not four yards away from me, and in quite calm water, I rose, hooked, and landed a fish of over a pound.

But what a fish! In the words of Long Murdo, the gillie, its back was 'black as tar.' Its belly was yellow, and its side bore a number of enormous spots. Never did a fish play less, and others we caught there played equally badly. From this I concluded that the trout were all old.

At the tail of the loch was a great bank of mud covered with moss and forming a natural dam. Through this a little water filtered into a tiny burn, which seemed to rise at the foot of the bank. A man by working an hour at this bank with a spade could have reduced the level of the loch by at least four feet.

There was no burn, so far as I could see, coming into the loch. It was therefore a reasonable conclusion that the trout which were in the loch when their exit was cut off by the collection of mud and moss, were the very ones we were catching. There was little or no chance for any to breed. In some years, perhaps, a great storm would sweep away the mud-bank, and then some fish would get out to breed and a few fresh ones come in; but I felt quite sure that the natural dam I saw had existed for ten or fifteen years, which would account for the peculiarities of the trout. Had there been breeding-grounds, and more fish in the loch, they would certainly have run much smaller.

I soon worked round to where Westbury was fishing, and found he had caught one trout of ¾lb. The rise appearing over, we decided, perhaps not very wisely, to try a loch we could see about a quarter of a mile distant. To get to it we had to cross some curious country, through which the rain had cut numbers of gullies, five feet or more in depth in the soft peat. An old cock grouse flew up with a whirr, and gave us a crowing welcome as we neared the loch. There seemed no fish moving, so we decided that lunch should be the next operation, after which we proceeded to fish Loch Cooish—I spell the word phonetically—or, the Loch of the Ear.

The water was very much lower than in the other loch, and the peat-banks rose about four feet in height, and were much undermined by the waves of the winter storms. The loch did not seem more than a few feet in depth anywhere, and there was an abundance of pale green grass-like weed, by the sides of which I rose several fish. The bottom was partly gravel and partly rock. W. and I separated as before.

In about half an hour I caught nine fish, which averaged a little over a third of a pound, but never in my life have I seen more lovely trout. They were as beautiful as the others were ugly. Short, thick fish, with silvery sides and brownish-pink backs. No two of them were spotted alike. Had I not seen char in other waters, I might have thought they were not trout at all. One half-pounder I caught ran quite ten yards of line off the reel as soon as hooked, and fought like a sea-trout.

It was interesting to compare the play afforded by these little fish with that of the large trout in the lake we had left. Not one of the latter, though going up to 2 lb., took an inch of line off the reel. In the Loch of the Ear the trout rose fitfully. Now and again there were showers, and just before the rain we were sure of a few rises. These fish knew no fear. Like the others, they seized the artificial insects in perfectly calm water, and I did not see a rise except to my flies; possibly because there was nothing else to rise at.

About two o'clock we left this beautiful water with some regret, so as to have an hour or two at the big trout of Ghrinnabhat. This time we stuck to the sheltered side of the loch, and fished close to the bank in calm water. I had on a large soldier palmer, and I found this a very good fly. In the course of an hour we took seven good trout, mostly over a pound, and one, as I have said, of 2 lb., which was caught by Westbury. For a short time I tried a Devon minnow, thinking it might lure a very large fish, but I did not get a run with it. I do not think a single fish was taken more than three yards from the shore. In most instances we saw the fish swim out from under the bank and take the fly.

I have often heard gillies say that in little-fished lochs the trout rise close to the bank, but that after the water has been whipped a few times it is necessary to cast further out for them. As to this, it may be remarked that a good deal must depend on the depth and configuration of the bottom of the loch.

About five o'clock we had to leave, as it was absolutely necessary to be off the moor before nightfall, owing to the walking being in places dangerous. We soon reached Loch Langabhat and found it a large but very shallow piece of water, the depth of which had evidently been artificially lowered. I took a few casts, but rose nothing. At that time of year it should have held some sea-trout, being connected by a burn with a considerable river. It was a loch which, by a little engineering, might be used to create an artificial spate in the salmon-river. At one end rose abruptly a great rock, and round its shores were dotted the shielings used by the milk-girls when the cows are kept on the moor in the summer. A very picturesque spot.

After leaving this last of the three lochs which we fished that day, we made our way down a valley, and came to some very boggy ground, in the centre of which was a small water-hole, measuring perhaps eighteen yards by three. The water was almost level with the moor. In the centre was a clump of rushes. Playing over it was a cloud of midges, and I saw what I at first thought was a dimple in the water, caused by a bubble of gas, rising from the muddy bottom. But the dimple was repeated not once, but twice.

'Surely never a trout in a spot like that?' I said.

Westbury laughed, and the gillie went on, little thinking any one would cast a fly in such a place. But my rod was still up, and it did not take a moment to release the cast which was wound round it. The tail fly was a very large Zulu, and this I lightly let fall on the water where I had last seen the dimple. In a moment a fish had it, and without attempting to play him I whipped out on to the bank a plump trout of over half a pound. I tried the water all over, but seemed to have caught its sole occupant.

It was the last place in the world to expect a trout, but it must be remembered we were in a land of underground burns.

'Why, the very puddles grow trout!' exclaimed Westbury.

Even this slight delay had been dangerous, for daylight was failing as we struck the old peat-wall. By the time we reached the green valley which had seemed such pleasant walking in the morning it was nearly dark, and we found it most difficult to avoid being bogged. By the kennels was Donald, anxiously waiting to see what we had brought from the loch of which he considered himself the discoverer. I could not resist saying, 'You sent us on a fool's errand, Donald,' but his face showed such great disappointment, that I at once lifted the lid of the creel, and the sight of the good fish therein made his face light up in a wonderful manner.

The trout were duly weighed, and so ended one of the most interesting and instructive day's fishing I have ever had in my life.

CHAPTER IX

'SALMO IRRITANS' AND HIS VANQUISHMENT

THIS variety of the salmon family, though not mentioned in any ichthyological work, is one with which many anglers are, unfortunately for themselves, only too well acquainted. When these fish rise the day is not marked with a red letter, but rather with a 'big, big D,' inscribed in the blackest ink. With the number of their fin rays and pyloric appendages, with the shape of their operculum, and with the exact position of their dorsal fin, the readers of these veracious lines need not be troubled, for in the following account of one day's salmon-fishing Frith and I had on the Gheira river, the distinguishing characteristics of the variety are sufficiently evident.

Hitherto sport had been anything but bad. Eight salmon which had risen to my fly had been duly creeled without disaster, and when one morning, after a trivial six-days' drought, Donald, the keeper, sent in word that there was a 'right spate' in the river, and that 'she' would fish well, our hopes were raised to the highest. We were then at the period of spring tides so favourable to a good run of fish, and salmon and seatrout in plenty had been seen leaping in the bay. So we rejoiced, ate our breakfasts hurriedly, and as soon after as possible, with no forebodings of the evils in store for us, started at a canter for the river, for is it not a tradition handed down through generations of keepers and gillies that the river cannot be fished too early, nor the lochs too late? but a tradition, by the way, which for some reason or other found little favour at Gheira.

We reached the waterside shortly after ten

'SALMO IRRITANS,' HIS VANQUISHMENT

o'clock, and found 'her' a wee bit dirty, perhaps, but at an exceedingly proper height.

Up to nearly the middle of September the best pools, which had been improved considerably by succeeding tenants, were those nearest the sea, and in these, under favourable conditions, two or three clean-run, silvery fish, varying in weight from five to ten or eleven pounds, might always be expected. Four of the pools lay in the rocky gorge described in Chapter IV. I took the lowest one, and Frith, my host's brother, took the third from the sea. To get at my water I had to climb a steep bank from which the pool my friend was fishing could be seen. Almost at the first cast he hooked a salmon, and I paused a moment to watch the fun. But there was no fun. At the end of two or three minutes his rod suddenly straightened. The fish, which had not shown itself, was off, certainly not through any fault of the fisherman, who had handled it with great care.

Then I began to fish, and at about the fourth

cast, in the tail of the run at the head of the pool, a salmon showed itself and seized the fly. Instead of making a rush on feeling the sting of the steel (query, do salmon feel any sting whatever?), it lay on the surface kicking and splashing, though given every opportunity to descend into deeper water, and at the end of four or five seconds away came the hook. Two salmon lost in the first ten minutes! We both of us gave the pools a long rest and tried them again, but to no purpose, and finding they apparently contained no more rising fish, went further up the river. Four pools were fished unsuccessfully, and when, about one o'clock, I waded out to a huge rock in the centre of the river—an excellent cast—it was without any expectation of rising another fish.

But in angling it is nearly always the unexpected which happens to us. After going twice over the pool, a salmon came at my small Jock Scot from behind two stones which were just breaking the surface of the water near the

'SALMO IRRITANS,' HIS VANQUISHMENT

tail of the pool. It was a large fish—that is, large for the river—and, as luck would have it, missed the fly altogether. After the orthodox rest, I tried him again, and as the fly swept into the eddy behind the stones, he came at it like a tiger. But on went the fly into the centre of the pool absolutely untouched. It is small satisfaction to write about this irritating fish. Suffice it to say, I devoted an hour and a half to him, tried various flies, and rose him four times, but did not feel him once.

Frith, who had not been more fortunate than I, now joined me, and we went some distance further up the gorge to the large, lake-like pool, which usually contains several fish when any are in the river. It was the pool from which Vernon conjured his eight fish in the masterly manner already recorded. Frith took one-half of the pool and I the other. There was only a slight ripple on it, so I put up a very small Black Doctor, and two fish, which would not permit me to hook them, seized the fly very gingerly under water. Having gone over the pool once, we had lunch, fished it again, and had two more short rises from salmon.

The water, which had fallen considerably, was now too low for us to go higher up the river, and we returned to the pools we had fished in the morning. From the big rock where I had spent so much time earlier in the day I rose another fish—a small one this time—and he, like his irritating fellow, rose as shortly as he came up frequently. Three times did he inspect my fly. Nothing seemed of any avail. Small flies were as futile as moderate-sized ones; while the larger sizes were of no use whatever. Light or dark, little or big, sober-coloured or gaudy, it was all the same to these peculiar fish. They would not take, though they would rise as frequently as the most exigent salmon-fisher could wish.

Late in the afternoon we met Vernon coming

'SALMO IRRITANS,' HIS VANQUISHMENT

up the river with a man who had just arrived. They had taken a few casts by the way. 'Any luck?' I queried. The new arrival looked down at his legs, which were smothered in red mud up to the knees, and drily replied—

'Yes.'

He had had one rise—and his luck consisted in walking into a bog which owed its moistness to an iron spring. I much regret I had not the opportunity of Kodaking his dry humorous expression as he regarded the somewhat dainty boots, etc., in which he had been travelling. Being the keenest of the keen where fish were concerned, he had only waited to unpack a rod, and had hurried up the river attired as he was.

Sometimes I did have my Kodak with me on such occasions, and obtained some very remarkable, if somewhat misleading, photographs with it. 'By the kind permission' (as the phrase runs) of the originals, I am able to give here a picture taken one day on the moor. It would

DAYS IN THULE

be a valuable piece of evidence in a breach of promise case, or an inquisition by the lunacy

'THEY DO LOOK AS IF THEY WERE DANCING A WILD JIG, DON'T THEY?'

commissioners—they do look as if they were dancing a wild jig, don't they? The whole

'SALMO IRRITANS,' HIS VANQUISHMENT

truth, and nothing but the truth, is, that the picture simply represents a very charming young lady being assisted up the side of a gully by a most gallant, attentive and kind gentleman. But *révenons à notre Salmo irritans.*

Our friends went a little distance up the river to the big pool, and I thought it might be advisable, the fish having had a long rest, to take a few more casts from the big rock. To my surprise the small salmon, or one about its size, and in the same spot, came again, and actually rose eight times without once touching the various flies I tried over him. This may seem incredible to some salmon-fishermen, but I can only say that I carefully counted the number of rises and have exaggerated nothing. Very much disgusted, we went back to the pools which we had fished in the morning, and there rose two salmon. One of these rose when I was fishing from the high bank some distance above the water, and I could distinctly see that it did not come within a foot of the fly. In the same pool I managed at last to catch one fish, a fresh-run sea-trout with sea-lice on it.

On the whole it was a noteworthy day's salmon-fishing: ten fish rose to our flies something like twenty-three times, and not one found its way into the creel; and if these fish did not belong to the variety *Salmo irritans*—well, the variety does not exist. On joining our host in the evening, we found that during the short time they fished he and the new arrival had similar experiences to ours; one salmon was hooked, but only for a few seconds, and several others were risen. All day long, though the water was falling, fish were running up, and we saw a good many making their way up the various falls below the principal pools. The day was dull, with occasional showers, and wind NW.

To rise ten salmon in a day without landing one would make any fisherman dissatisfied with his tackle and himself. After mature reflection

'SALMO IRRITANS,' HIS VANQUISHMENT

I came to the conclusion that ordinary salmon flies were of little use for *Salmo irritans*, and that

'SOMETHING SPECIALLY DIABOLICAL.'

for him something specially diabolical must be devised. By the following morning's post diagrams of flies with most fearful and wonderful double hooks, and carefully drawn-up directions, were sent to Warner's, the Redditch hook-makers, who carried out my orders to the letter. In the meantime the river, of course, more or less dried up.

It was some time before I had an opportunity of testing the contrivance (to be presently described) which I had invented to bring about the destruction of *Salmo irritans*. On the first day that there was a slight rise of water in the river, my friend of the iron bog and I journeyed some five or six miles up-stream (the lower pools being occupied) to fish at Joanna's pool, which was said to contain several salmon. The day was bright, the higher we ascended the river the lower was the water, and on arriving at our destination we found hardly a ripple on the pool. The outlook was as bad as possible. My friend, using the ordinary flies, did not have a single rise. I put up a fiery brown dressed on the new hooks, and at the very first cast a fish took it under water —a fine hen salmon of $11\frac{1}{2}$lb., which had been some little time in fresh water, but was still in the pink of condition. I did not get another rise; but to catch a fish at all under such unfavourable circumstances was very encouraging, and spoke well for the invention. The vanquishment of *Salmo irritans* had commenced.

The day on which the new hooks were most

'SALMO IRRITANS,' HIS VANQUISHMENT

thoroughly tested was at the beginning of October, and appeared too bright for successful salmon-fishing. The river had fallen somewhat. Wind NWW., a blue sky, with occasional showers coming over the hills from the Atlantic. Probably, had I not been anxious to utilise every chance of meeting with my old enemy *Salmo irritans*, I should have deserted the river for the grouse moor.

The best pool anywhere near the lodge was being fished by my host, so we (the we consisting of Long Murdo and myself) decided to try some of the higher pools. I may mention here that my host rose six fish or more, but only landed one, so I have some reason for supposing that the fish were rising short. On the way up, Kennie, the river-watcher, joined us, and I was glad of his company, as, being day and night by the river, he knew nearly every fish in every pool.

On the open moorland, a couple of miles or more from the sea, the river makes a sharp bend, and by eating into a peat-bank has worked out a fairly deep pool. Here, according to tradition, a former tenant landed eleven fish in one day; but now the pool has filled up somewhat, and two salmon are the most any one can expect to get out of it. I began fishing at this noted spot, putting up a small fiery brown on the new hooks. But no rise rewarded my efforts, and we passed on to a pool at another bend in the river, where history does not record the capture of a single salmon, but which always holds a fish or two. It would have been all the better for a good ripple, but two big rocks broke the water slightly.

'Tell me exactly where the fish lie, Kennie.'

'Weel, it's joost there, between the big stones, whatever,' replied Kennie; and sure enough, at the second cast there uprose a salmon, which seized the fly and went away up stream into the pool above. It was an easy matter to follow him, and he should have been killed in ten

'SALMO IRRITANS,' HIS VANQUISHMENT

minutes; but Long Murdo was somewhat unhandy with the gaff, and kept pecking at the fish as if he was using a pickaxe. However, all's well that ends well, and it was no small satisfaction to see a fish which had had every chance of escape given it fairly gaffed at last. He was hooked in the tongue.

Leaving the two pools, we walked about half a mile higher to a small gorge, down which the river makes a series of leaps, forming several good casts for salmon. They are known as the Steps pools. I commenced at the topmost one, which was long and narrow; but finding the water too heavy for my small fly, put up one slightly larger and brighter, a Jock Scot tied on one of the new hooks, with the bend the same as before, the shank only being enlarged for the larger fly.

But even the Jock Scot was too small for the water at this part of the river, and I unfortunately had on that day no larger flies dressed on the new hooks. So the Steps pools produced nothing, and leaving them, we pushed still further up stream to a small but good holding pool, by the side of which stood the walls of a small shieling. In the Shieling pool there was a salmon—so Kennie the watcher said; and Kennie was right, for about the second or third cast a very nearly fresh-run fish, which was lying under a projecting rock on the other side of the river, caught sight of my Jock Scot, followed it across the stream, and seized it in shallow water, almost at my feet. Had I not been kneeling, that fish would probably have refused the fly. After some gallant play, it was neatly gaffed by Murdo, and proved to be an almost fresh-run hen.

Still working up-stream, I fished two other small pools without a rise, and at two o'clock cried a halt for lunch, which we enjoyed in a little heather-grown dell close to the water. The men were some twenty yards distant, and I was eating away in solitary state, when who should pay me a visit but a blue mountain-hare, akin perhaps to those amiable creatures Alice met in Wonderland, which came ambling up in the most unconcerned manner within five yards or so of where I was sitting. Immediately I saw it I remained perfectly motionless, and the hare, having regarded me for a few seconds without the slightest appearance of fear, and without making any audible remark, trotted off quietly and unconcernedly.

It is very curious how little fear the shyest of wild animals have of human beings so long as they do not move. I have noticed the same thing of fish. Once, when standing on the towpath of the Thames watching the minnows at play, three great chub, each about 5 lb. in weight, swam up slowly out of the deep water right up to my feet, and began cruising about as if looking for food. I remained still for some minutes watching them, but a slight movement of my hand sent them off post-haste to the deep hole whence they had wandered.

On the way down the river after lunch I tried the Steps pool with a Lion, dressed on rather large double hooks; but I was punished for deserting the new pattern, which had served me so well. In the lowest of the pools a larger fish rose and missed the fly. After a rest he seized the fly under water, gave a plunge, and was off. My next attempt was made in the pool in which I had begun fishing in the morning. Unfortunately I had kept up the fly dressed on the large double hook (the Lion), and a curious thing happened.

The fish lie under the far side of the pool, in about four or five feet of water. On the near side the river runs very shallow, and about ten feet from the shore are two small stones, about as big as a horse's head, which on this occasion just showed above the water. The fly, which had been cast right against the peat bank on the opposite side, had fallen into the water just

'SALMO IRRITANS,' HIS VANQUISHMENT

where I expected a salmon to lie, and slowly swept round with the stream, until the line came over the two small stones just mentioned. Then the fly apparently caught in the stone, and I gave a vigorous flick with the rod to release it. But as it was still fixed in something, I tried a somewhat harder flick, then a salmon showed first its head and then its tail out of the water, and I found, to my own and Murdo's very great surprise, that I was fast in a good fish, which showed no inclination to move from behind the stone. The second jerk I had given had been hard enough to drag the fly out of the mouth of any fish which was lightly hooked, and I felt absolutely certain of getting this really fine salmon.

'You shall land this one,' was my unfortunate remark to Kennie, who was never so happy as when using the gaff. Was it the remark, or those large double hooks? It matters little which, for suddenly the fly came quietly away in the most unreasonable and aggravating manner.

The salmon was, I think, a female; and the moral, of course, is, *Never make cocksure of a hen fish.*

Though my Lion was rising fish, I would have no more of it, and put up the Jock Scot dressed on the small-bend, long-shanked double hook. With this, in a pool a little lower down, I hooked a cock fish which, in Kennie's words, was 'as wild as a deer.' I killed him half a dozen times over, but every time, as he came just within reach of the gaff, he realised his position and dashed off to the other side of the river. Kennie, who was anxious to distinguish himself, became excited; and, seeing this, I bade him use a landing-net we had brought with us on the chance of meeting with sea-trout. The end of it was that the fish suddenly bolted down stream, and, passing over a shallow where his back was out of water, Kennie rushed in below him and caught him neatly in the net. That ended the day's fishing.

'SALMO IRRITANS,' HIS VANQUISHMENT

Salmon-fishers may like to know something further of the peculiar hooks referred to, and for them alone the following lines are intended. I advise every one else to proceed at once to the next chapter.

The difficulty was to devise a hook which would penetrate and hold on those occasions when the ordinary hook of commerce would merely scratch. In the ordinary salmon-fly the end of the wing and the curve of the hook are about level, so that, to get hooked, the salmon has to take rather more than half the fly in its mouth. I imagined, and have seen no reason to change my belief, that when one feels merely a pluck, the salmon has seized only the latter half of the fly, or less, or the fly has perhaps been properly seized but has been swimming on its side, and thus slipped sideways out of the fish's mouth without the point of the hook coming in contact with any part of the jaw. For this evil a double hook seems to be the natural remedy; but fish are probably not often lost from this reason if the angler takes every care to see that his cast is straight, especially near the fly, and that his fly swims properly.

The question with me was how to hook salmon which may seize the tail end of the fly. Clearly, the hook should project beyond the tail of the fly so far that if the fish seized only the tip of the wing the point of the hook would be within his mouth. But clearly, also, the hook must be kept small, for if large it would appear to be a portion of the fly, and the short rising fish might only seize the bend of the hook, or not rise at all to a small fly dressed on a large clumsy hook. Therefore the hook must be small—that is to say, *small in the bend, though long in the shank, and not unnecessarily heavy in the wire.*

But inasmuch as a hook with a small bend was apt to miss taking hold in a mouth so large as that possessed by the salmon, I decided to have them made double, but also had some flies

'SALMO IRRITANS,' HIS VANQUISHMENT

dressed on single hooks to experiment with. As regards these latter, I did not try them on salmon,[1] but I rose eight sea-trout on them, of which I caught six. Sea-trout are such notorious short-risers that for the hook to project well beyond the fly may prove to be a very decided advantage.

With regard to the new hooks, I rarely used anything else for salmon on the five days I was able to fish after receiving them. I had several flies (Jock Scotts, doctors, lions, fiery browns, etc.), tied in three different sizes, the bend of the hook being kept one size, the shank only varying in length. The makers sent me some flies tied on rather larger double hooks, but, after losing two fish on these, I gave them up for those with the very small bend. The shank of the hook, as I have already said, projected considerably beyond the tail of the flies, and it seemed impossible that

[1] At least not then. I have killed one or two fish with them since.

any fish which seized any part of the fly could avoid getting hooked. In these five days' fishing, when using the long-shanked, small bend, double hooks, I touched eleven fish and landed ten, a result which is, of course, not impossible with the ordinary single hook, but speaks very well for the new shape.

It is a grand thing to have one's name handed down to posterity as the discoverer of a new member of the *Salmonidæ* family. I first announced the event in the *Field*, where it created much interest. Men I had not heard of for years wrote to me about the strange fish or the new hooks to catch him with. Some claimed to have discovered him before I was born, but that was mere jealousy, and they produced no evidence. The creature was even glorified (or cussed) in verse, Mr. Andrew Lang writing a short poem on him for the Christmas Number of the *Fishing Gazette*. Mr. Lang kindly allows me to reprint his amusing verses :—

THE *SALMO IRRITANS*

BY ANDREW LANG

I.

A most accommodating fish
  Is he who lies in stream or pot,
Who rises frequent as you wish
  At Silver Doctor or Jock Scott
  Or any other fly you've got
In all the piscatory clans;
  You strike, but ah! you strike him not:
He is the *Salmo irritans*.

II.

You give him the accustomed rest;
  A quarter of an hour or so—
And then you cast your very best,
  Your heart is throbbing, loud or low,
He rises with a splendid show
  Of silver side and fins like fans,
Perchance you think you've got him? No!
  He is the *Salmo irritans*.

III.

You leave him till the eventide,
  When wandering on by dub and pool
A score of other casts you've tried,
  All fruitless and all beautiful;

DAYS IN THULE

But *he* still rises, calm and cool,
   Who is not yours, nor any man's!
He leaves you looking like a fool:
   He is the *Salmo irritans*.

IV.

Prince, wherefore comes he *always* short,
   This demon whom the angler bans?
This is his selfish view of sport,
   He is the *Salmo irritans* !

CHAPTER X

THE RABBITS OF THE CLIFFS

N some parts of its coast-line the island yields a remarkable variety of sport. The sea swarms with cod, hake, haddock, herrings, and other fish in their seasons; in the caves and crannies of the coast are great flocks of blue rock-pigeons, which afford perhaps the most difficult shooting in Britain; seals are by no means uncommon, and among the cliffs dwell immense and ever-increasing colonies of rabbits. Sea-birds of many kinds are there in myriads, but these, of course, possess more interest for the naturalist than for the mere sportsman.

Rabbits were, I believe, introduced by the late

Sir James Matheson. They are found of many colours, from black to white with black markings. Many have dark rings round their necks, and some seem to be reverting to the original type. With them are great numbers of the ordinary wild rabbit. The black ones, it seemed to me, were much more shy and difficult to get at than any of the others. In places the shooting consists of merely making a detour to get to the top of some high rocky point of land and potting the rabbits as they feed below; but those portions of the cliffs where the rabbits are most plentiful are, it need hardly be said, the least accessible, and the shooting is of quite another kind.

Among the bent-covered sand-hills by the sea rabbits have made their homes. Here they are often found lying out, and some fair shooting may be had by walking the bent; and there is, of course, some ferreting to be done in the burrows. But among the cliffs ferreting is

THE RABBITS OF THE CLIFFS

out of the question, nor is any dog, except a very steady retriever, of the least use.

What may be termed the cliff rabbit-shooting was simply delightful work. The surroundings were romantic and picturesque in the extreme, the rabbits afforded every possible variety of shots, and there was just that spice of danger in stalking them which always adds so much to the enjoyment of any kind of sport.

One day late in September we organised an expedition against the rabbits, combined with a picnic on the sands for the benefit of the ladies. The day commenced with an eight-mile drive along a moorland road, through the glorious Hebridean air, keen and invigorating, and not quite so evanescent in its effects as champagne.

On the way we passed two strapping crofters' girls who, with feet bare, were stepping smartly out on their way to do some shopping in Stornoway. A little matter of twenty-two miles there and home again. One of them had thrown back the peculiar head-dress which they mostly wear

'A LITTLE MATTER OF TWENTY-TWO MILES THERE AND HOME AGAIN!'

as a protective in that windy and wet part of the kingdom.

Leaving the moor we passed through the great peat-bog which affords fuel to the inhabitants

THE RABBITS OF THE CLIFFS

of those curious crofter townships peculiar to the Lews. Just on the edge of the bog was a picturesque group consisting of an old crofter

'A PICTURESQUE GROUP.'

or fisherman-farmer, a weather-beaten, smoke-dried, sturdy woman, attired in the dress of the country, and a sleek cow, which the man was leading about by a halter. I was fortunate in being able to obtain a good photograph of this interesting little scene. The illustration shows very clearly the soleless stocking which the women wear. The country is too wet for leather boots, and (most of the year) too cold for bare legs. This peculiar stocking is a compromise.

A mile beyond the crofters' cottages we came to a farmhouse belonging to a Yorkshireman whose father had migrated, Heaven knows why, to these solitudes years before. Here we put up the horses, and those who were least desirous of climbing devoted themselves to the burrows among the sand-dunes, while two guns, Gerald and myself, were told off to storm the cliffs.

It is not easy to picture the great beauty of the scene in which we found ourselves. Down a heather-clad valley which narrowed into a rocky gorge babbled a little burn which, after spreading over the pure white sands of a bay a furlong or more in width, mingled with the low breakers caused by a gentle swell rolling in from

THE RABBITS OF THE CLIFFS

the Atlantic. Rising out of the sands were lofty rocks, on one of which a pirate's castle stood in years gone by. From half-tide up to high water it was quite surrounded by the sea.

The sands were closed in on each side by dark cliffs haunted by the green shag and seagulls. Above the cliffs were slopes covered with fine, sweet grass, kept short as on any lawn by the sheep and rabbits. A little above high-water mark, and at the foot of a second tier of rocky heights which faced and closed in the bay, except for the valley through which ran the burn, was a shallow loch covered with water-lilies, and fringed with reeds.

The face of these inland cliffs, over which heather and bracken grew luxuriantly, was rugged and broken. At their base were piled up great heaps of moss-covered rocks, some of them many tons in weight. Rabbits in thousands dwelt among these masses of fallen rock, but were not easily shot. Even when feeding in the evening it was rare to find one any distance from some nook or cranny into which he could bolt on hearing a footstep.

During the morning Gerald and I worked the inner cliffs with results little better than those obtained by the ferreters on the dunes. It took some time to collect every one for lunch, and afterwards there seemed a general indisposition to do anything but bask in the September sunshine, and enjoy the beauties of the place. Truth to say, a late lunch often means too hearty a meal, followed, if not by a disposition towards indolence, by somewhat indifferent shooting. A seal disporting itself in almost human fashion in the surf induced Gerald and me to steal down to the shore for a closer inspection. But we could get no nearer to it than seventy yards, and having no rifle with us, would not hazard a shot, except with the camera, which resulted in a picture of a low rocky point and surf breaking on the sand, but no seal. The beautiful creature,

ever careful to keep its distance, fished steadily among the breakers, now and again standing almost upright in the water to look at us, exposing about a third of its body.

After watching it for a while I suggested a stroll along the cliffs, where none of us had yet been. Gerald assented, and we had hardly left the bay before a black rabbit dashed out of a clump of bracken at our feet. I fired, but he ran fifty yards and disappeared under a heap of stones. I imagined it was a clean miss, but Gerald thought otherwise. On examining the heap of stones I saw a spot of blood on one of them, put my arm in, and pulled out the rabbit quite dead. It had been shot in the head.

Gradually ascending we found ourselves a considerable height above the sea, so made our way by a sheep-track along the face of the cliff, and entered upon a veritable land of rabbits. We saw no seals. Numbers of blue rock-pigeons darted by us, but we did not attempt to shoot

THE RABBITS OF THE CLIFFS

any, as they were all flying over the sea, and could not have been retrieved. The rabbits, therefore, engrossed our attention. There was hardly a rock under which we did not see a white tail vanishing as we advanced cautiously. Snapshots were the only ones possible, and our foothold being anything but secure, there was a certain amount of powder burned without much effect. None the less we soon killed more rabbits than it was convenient to carry, and we regretted we had not brought a gillie with us. Moreover, we required a guide, for more than once, after an anything but pleasant scramble over great boulders and loose stones, we found ourselves stopped by some miniature precipice, and had to retrace our steps. As we could not possibly carry the dead rabbits and continue shooting, we hid those we had killed under a stone and went on our way.

Presently we came to a grassy slope at the edge of which the rock went down straight to the sea, about a hundred feet below. Some rabbits were out feeding, and one of them I shot before he could get to his stronghold. The place was shut in on both sides by steep rocks, round which it was just possible to climb by a sheep-path leading to some broken ground where, to all appearance, one gun would probably do more execution than two. So I left Gerald to work the place by himself. He had hardly turned the corner before he fired, and I heard his gun repeatedly during the next ten minutes.

Meanwhile I sat on the springy turf, thankful for the rest, and watched a great solan goose making his wonderful dives from giddy heights with folded wings, head foremost into the sea. Up would fly froth and foam as he struck the water, and a second or two later he would bounce up like a cork, as often as not without the fish he had aimed at. Presently a rabbit ambled out on to the grass at the edge of the slope and began feeding. I fired, and unfortunately did not hit it sufficiently hard to prevent it gaining a burrow under a large stone.

It was a curious thing, but these rabbits took little notice of the report of a gun. I noticed on several occasions that after shooting over a particular piece of ground, if we walked it again a quarter of an hour later, we probably found nearly as many rabbits out as before. As a matter of fact, these cliffs are so little shot over, in some seasons not at all, that the rabbits probably do not associate the noise of guns with an attack on themselves.

Not five minutes had elapsed before another rabbit made its appearance and commenced calmly browsing on the short sweet herbage. I would not again hazard a shot at that distance, having a strong dislike to wound game and allow it to die a slow and painful death. So I stole down the slope to get nearer. That most confiding creature fed on and never noticed me. At thirty yards I fired and the result was tragic, I may say melodramatic. The poor thing rolled over, lay still for a second, rolled again, and always nearing with each struggle the brink of the cliff. Almost as I seized him, he made one last effort and went over the edge out of sight. There was a sickening thud on a projecting rock, and a splash in the water below. I felt like the murderer in an Adelphi melodrama or shilling shocker, or rather I should say that I felt myself on an equality with those inhuman monsters.

The deed of horror was just over when Gerald returned with several couple of rabbits, saying he could have shot many more but was afraid that if he did so they would fall off the cliffs into the sea.

Having made another pile of rabbits, we continued our scramble, getting a shot here and another there, until we came to a spot where, even for a goat, there was no possible foothold. A great natural obelisk, split from the mainland by some convulsion of nature, rose up out of the sea, and the wall of rock, from which it had

THE RABBITS OF THE CLIFFS

parted centuries ago, went down sheer to the water's edge. There was nothing for us but to ascend to the moor above. This we had no reason to regret, for, as our heads appeared suddenly above the cliff-top, we caught sight of a hundred or more rabbits all feeding within gunshot. They were as much astonished as we were. Some clearly lost their heads, bolting hither and thither, and gave us the opportunity of reloading and firing again after emptying our barrels at them. On going up to collect the killed and wounded, I kicked up still another rabbit and shot him.

Beyond this point the country did not look very promising, so we turned and made our way along the tops of the cliffs towards the farmhouse. Several times we had to make more or less perilous descents to recover our dead rabbits, and, what with the heavy load and the climb among the crags, loose stones, and moist, slippery places, which were worst of all, we had had quite enough by the time we reached the abode of our Yorkshire friend.

Night had fallen, and we found that the merry picnic party had given us up and driven off an hour earlier, leaving the head-keeper to bring us home behind an aged pony, almost as used-up as we were. The cows had not been milked, but Bridget, the dairymaid, blessings be on her, broke her cream for us, and gave us that finest of restoratives, fresh milk and good Scotch whisky in equal parts. After which, much refreshed, we bade the worthy farmer and his wife farewell, and set out on our long, dark, and cold drive over the lonesome moor.

CHAPTER XI

OUR SEA-TROUT DITCH

IT is, perhaps, an unkind thing to speak of a piece of water which is dignified on the Ordnance Survey by the name of a river, as a ditch, but a channel four feet deep and ten feet wide, which winds through a swamp, and contains water in which there is no perceptible stream, can hardly rank among rivers. It is the last place in the world in which one would expect to get good fishing; but 'at times,' as the guide-books say, some very fine baskets of both brown and sea-trout can be caught out of it. It rises somewhere up in the moorlands—a pretty little rill, flowing sometimes underground, at others twisting and twirling between peat banks, doing a desperate fall over a rocky ledge at least three feet wide and four feet high, and forming pools below almost as large as a full-sized sponge-bath. Reaching the valley, it broadens out into a swampy lagoon, not more than eighteen inches deep in any part, and between this lagoon and the sea is the ditch referred to.

Though comparatively shallow, the water is so stained as to appear of unknown depth, and nowhere is the black peaty bottom visible. From the lagoon to the sea the distance is perhaps a quarter of a mile. Here it was that during spring tides fine shoals of sea-trout came to feed, returning, I venture to think, to the sea after spending perhaps four or five days in fresh water. Later on in the season, of course, they pushed up from the sea through the lagoon and into the moorland burn for spawning purposes.

There were ladies of our party who were

OUR SEA-TROUT DITCH

anxious to become fly-fishers, and the wise old keeper said that the river Colso was just the place for them. 'It had varra nice fishing whatefer, and the troots were plenty, and they rose varra well indeed whenefer there was a goot wind blowing up the strath.' So one morning I was commissioned to take two ladies to this curious piece of water.

The day commenced with a pleasant drive of a few miles along the breezy road round the bay in the direction of Stornoway. We left the dog-cart in the solid stone house belonging to a worthy sheepfarmer, John H——, around whose homestead was an expanse of excellent grass-land, on which the crofters cast envious eyes. On either side of the little path which led up to the door was a profusion of flowers. Indeed the worthy John, or his little daughter, 'Mary-Jo' (so called, perhaps, to distinguish her from some other Mary on whom the name of Joanna had not been conferred), had apparently bought packets of annual seeds, mixed their contents together, and sown them broadcast.

I have a vivid recollection of three little scenes at the farm-house: That gorgeous avenue of flowers, and Mrs. H—— standing in, and fairly filling the doorway beyond, beaming upon the arrivals. Then one October night a weary duck-shooter coming off the moor wet and exhausted, and being served with whisky and new milk in the old kitchen by Mary-Jo, the rest of the family gathered around. Lastly, John H—— standing outside in the sunshine, and commenting on the value of a certain mare he thought would suit Vernon.

'She's joost a fine mare,' he was saying, as I took his photograph.

But on this occasion we delayed not to photograph or discuss horses, but walked quickly down to the little stream which wound through the valley below. During the morning I played gillie—tied on flies that were whipped off every

OUR SEA-TROUT DITCH

five minutes, and officiated with the landing-net whenever a quarter-pounder was hooked. It is

'SHE'S JOOST A FINE MARE,' HE WAS SAYING.

impossible to give a better idea of the numbers and ignorance of the trout than by saying that during the day, if my memory errs not, these two ladies, who were absolute beginners in the art of fly-fishing, caught something like nine dozen fish. Here and there the breeze touched the water, but the fish rose in the calms as well as in those places where there was a ripple.

Towards the mouth of the ditch was a gravelly bar, which was very useful in keeping up the water, but tended to keep out the sea-trout except during spring tides. Below this bar was a little tidal pool; and towards the evening, while my companions were resting, I made a few casts here, and soon pulled out a couple of brace of finnocks. This led to inquiries, and it appeared that there were ancient traditions concerning this water of sea-trout, 'varra large and plenty,' as Donald would say, so when, therefore, there was a chance we fished the ditch for an hour or two, and at last we were rewarded.

OUR SEA-TROUT DITCH

I was not of the party which first happened on the sea-trout, having that day been fishing on one of the hundred or more lochs at our disposal. My friends, who had been fishing the ditch, had unfortunately gone only provided with the finest of tackle, intending to have made a great raid upon the little brown trout, but it seems that these were not rising and the sea-trout were, and the loss of flies was truly terrible. However, they brought some good trout home, but were loud in their lamentations concerning the still better fish that they had lost, several of them believed to be well over three pounds.

Later on, provided with flies tied on something stronger than gossamer gut, we fished the place, and, though its occupants were neither rising so freely nor appeared to be so plentiful as on the previous occasion, we killed a good basketful. In a little water like this, where, owing to the muddy bottom, wading was impossible, it was extremely difficult to keep out of sight of the fish. To cast up-stream was absolutely necessary, and the flies most favoured were small, one in particular, which was great medicine, was a red and black hackle, the pattern for which was given me by Dr. Hamilton, author of those delightful *Recollections of Salmon, Trout, and Grayling Fishing*. It was dressed thus:—

At the head a good-sized black hackle; the half of the body next the hackle rough crimson pig's wool; the tail half of the body of bright golden brown pig's wool; and the tail, a topping.

Dressed very small, this fly proved most attractive to the little brown trout of the Colso ditch, and the day on which was made the biggest bag of brown trout of the season, most of the fish were caught on it. It was a really good all-round fly, best of all for sea-trout, but attractive to salmon and brown trout in peat-stained waters. I think it was Major Traherne who pointed out that in coffee-coloured waters one requires for salmon a fly that can be seen by the fish—a truism which is sometimes overlooked—and that from experiments he had made, he discovered that a fly in which scarlet and black were contrasted was the most showy of all. This fly of Dr. Hamilton's, therefore, is particularly suited for rivers which take their rise in peat-bogs.

One day when I visited the Colso ditch there was no wind, and a most dazzling sun; the fish by that time had become somewhat educated, and I found myself reduced to the necessity of fishing with a dry fly. There was nothing rising so far as one could see, probably for the reason that there was nothing to rise at, which is a very ordinary state of affairs on northern rivers.

After vainly whipping the water with a cast of flies worked in the ordinary fashion, I thought I would try what a Hampshire dun would do, put one up, and made a few casts up-stream. I soon came upon a fish which, though of an inquiring disposition, had considerable difficulty in making up his mind to take the fly. Perhaps he could not see it through the peaty water so well as he desired, for the first thing he did was to leap lightly over it, no doubt squinting at it while on his way through the air. I tried another cast, and he rose and missed. The third time he was fast, and proved to be a black-backed little youngster of a quarter of a pound.

Further up the lagoon I rose a half-pounder, and never did angler and fish have such a game of cast and rise as did we two that sunny afternoon. He was clearly unaccustomed to taking flies on the surface, though he had a natural tendency in that direction. Possibly he had some obliqueness of vision. However that may be, he tried for a good quarter of an hour to take that fly before succeeding. He was lying at the edge of a few reeds; my fly would fall just over his nose, and up he would come six inches to the right or left of it; another cast, he would be well in front of it; and still another, he would miss it by six inches. I lost all count of the number of times I rose him, but finally he did succeed in getting it in his mouth, and having got it there, instead of being pleased, as he ought to have been after taking so much trouble to secure it, dashed up-stream, turned a somersault in the air, jiggered like any salmon, and did his very utmost to get rid of the hook. He was a plump, shapely half-pounder, which, from his handsome colour, had just returned from a visit to the tidal-pool. In September the fishing fell off in the ditch, any sea-trout coming into it no doubt pushing up the burn, but few of us had any time to wield the rod, war having broken out between the occupants of the lodge and the grouse. Still, on off days, when dogs and men were resting, we would go down to the Colso and get a few of these hungry little brownies, and now and again a sea-trout. But I never could get over my feelings of astonishment at obtaining good sport in such a queer place.

CHAPTER XII

FAREWELL TO THULE

'SAY, there's a deuce of a swell outside talking to Donald,' said Gerald one morning, on coming in from a visit to the kennels. 'Who is he?'

No one knew, and every one felt interested, for, with the exception of the crofter's cots and a farm, there was not a house within nine miles of us. A few minutes later I came upon our visitor and found that Gerald's description of him, though slightly lacking in detail, was broadly accurate enough. He was a tall, fair, good-looking youth of twenty summers or more, with freckled face and bright blue eyes. He was clad in new tweeds with knickerbocker breeches, light spats, and shining shoes. There was a horsey-looking little scarf, too, held in position by a gold pin.

Where had he dropped from? In due course Donald solved the mystery. It, or I should say he, was the piper from the other side of the island who had trotted fifteen miles across the roadless moor (surely bearing those shoes and spats under his arm), and was going to rouse the echoes at the gillies' ball in the evening. But where were the tartan and fillibeg, where the cap and eagle's feather? Where that finery which makes the Scotch piper a thing beauteous to look upon?

However, I discovered that our blue-eyed friend could not rightly wear such apparel, not being quite the real thing, but a sturdy young gamekeeper who had a 'gift with the pipes.' Some days previously I had seen a real piper, the one specially retained by the deceased laird. He, poor fellow, was on his way from his wife's funeral, and was clad in black broadcloth just like any one else. I have seen many more Highland pipers in all their beauty in London than elsewhere.

True to its tradition, Gheira Lodge was to open its doors to farmers, keepers, gillies, and watchers, with their spouses present and prospective. The pipes were to pipe, and reels were to be reeled. These festivities were to be the culminating joys of our visit to Thule.

The guests, I suppose, collected outside the lodge, for about nine o'clock the blue-eyed keeper marched in with pipes playing, Donald walking in front as a sort of M.C. leading the way to the roomy kitchen, the rest following. Donald then said a lengthy and impressive grace, and a well-sustained attack was made on the various excellent dishes and compounds prepared by the admirable Katie, who, beaming graciously on every one, played the hostess at the lower end of the table, Donald facing her. I only had a glimpse of these things.

At half-past ten Ina came in, bearing word that the guests were waiting for Vernon to make a speech to them, whereupon we all marched into the kitchen and were given glasses of wine. It was an interesting little ceremony. Vernon said just the right things, and pleased everybody, and Donald replied quietly and effectively. So well did he do it that I ventured to think he had played the *rôle* before. 'He had never been out with better sportsmen,' he said, 'and had never passed a happier season. He had fished for salmon many years, and thought he knew all about it, but was bound to say that I—J. B.—had shown him many things he did not know before. They were all sorry we were leaving the lodge, and looked forward to our return the following year.

I venture here to interpose the expression of a wish that the reader will not be too utterly disgusted at my most obvious and intense conceit in recording the compliment paid me by Donald.

But praise from a Highlander, coupled with the admission of having learned anything from an Englander, is almost unexampled. Let me confess, however, that the most Donald acquired from me was the use of a few novelties in fishing-tackle, a knot or two, and some facts about the natural history of fish well known to those who have even an elementary knowledge of ichthyology, but not to be learned by mere residence by a salmon-river.

Certainly I could not have made Donald a better fisherman than he was, for he cast a long, straight line, knew exactly how to work and where to place his fly, and was second to none in the use of the gaff. The only time I ever knew him fail was in an attempt to gaff a fish with a hake-hook tied on to a rough stick none too tightly with a boot-lace. He lost my salmon for me, but failure under such circumstances was pardonable.

After Donald had concluded his neat and complimentary speech, and our healths had been drunk, Sandy, the second keeper, who had done service with 'Sixty-Three,'[1] and was regarded and spoken of by the ladies of our party as a 'dear old man,' made a nice little speech, in which he said that he too had passed a happy season.

Then our little conjurer of salmon, Kennie, was called on by Vernon, and after a considerable amount of pressing and many expostulations in Gaelic, got on his legs, smiles rippling all over his merry face. He began with the usual 'Oh, ay,' paused a second or two, and then sensibly added that he had little English and could not make a speech, that he would have made one an he could.

After this the kiltless piper played us into another room, where all arranged themselves on benches round the walls, leaving as much space

[1] The Rev. C. Hutchinson, a great fisherman and shot, who spent some years in the Lews, and under this pseudonym published many capital articles in *The Field* on Hebridean Sport. Poor Sandy will pass no more happy seasons in this world. I heard of his death while this book was in the press.

as possible for the dancing. There was a little hesitation at the outset, and the piper's eye looked anxiously about as if its owner was wondering how long he was to be kept blowing wind into that skin for no purpose. But Donald was equal to the occasion and soon arranged a reel, which was danced in very solemn fashion.

Sitting demurely against the wall, with mittened hands crossed in their laps, were the belles of the ball, two sisters from a neighbouring village. One of these sang an old Scotch song very sweetly, after which our kind hostess thrilled these good people of Thule by singing 'The Last Rose of Summer' as, perhaps, it had never before been sung in the Hebrides. Another reel followed, and we left Donald and Katie to entertain the guests.

From time to time some of us looked in to view the scene, which grew gayer as the night wore on. Once we found that the young keeper had relinquished his pipes and was briskly dancing a reel with his shoes off, to do it the better. Not that the dancers were at any time musicless, for was not the policeman a notable performer on the accordion, and, when both piper and policeman were weary, did not the solemn Murdo produce a comb and a piece of paper, to which the dancers reeled as smartly as ever! But that was late in the evening, when no one was critical.

One strange thing dwells in my memory, an odious sacrifice on the Altar of Fashion, to wit, a polka played on the pipes! There was also an incident upon which I will not dilate, connected with the intrusion of an uninvited guest, of great activity, but questionable honesty.

In the small hours of the morning the guests dwindled reluctantly away, and if some could not have walked a chalk line, why, you know, one's legs are a wee shaky after dancing reels for six or seven hours.

Thus ended the ball. The two following days

were devoted to catching a badly-conditioned salmon or two for kippering at Stornoway, killing a few brace of grouse to be stored in the freezing chambers at Leadenhall Market for the Christmas festivities, and that most odious business generally termed 'packing-up.' The farewell-bidding to all the good people who had helped to make our visit to Thule so enjoyable was a sad affair. Long Murdo and, for once, Kennie looked simply miserable. On the road troops of young urchins, brown as to their faces, legs, and arms, raced after the dogcarts until they could run no more. Pleasant-looking women, who, I suspect, had benefited by kind Mrs. Vernon's liberality, stood at their doors and sent parting smiles after us. Frith took a photo of one little roadside scene, which he kindly allows me to reproduce.

There was a large party to dine and sleep in Stornoway at the Royal Hotel that evening, for the steamers which cross the Minch invariably

'FRITH TOOK A PHOTO OF ONE LITTLE ROADSIDE SCENE.'

start at most inconvenient hours. Gerald and I proposed to sleep on board the steamer, but on my asking for berths for us, the steward flatly refused us any accommodation, saying that the Stornoway people (hotel-keepers, I suppose, he meant) would not like it. He, moreover, displayed his classical attainments by informing me that his rules were those of the Medes and Persians.

This was the first incident in our return to town life. The proprietor of the hotel, Mackenzie, an ex-gamekeeper, was a thoroughly good fellow. When I told him of the steward's extraordinary behaviour, he said it was all nonsense, and went with me on board. But the Persian ruler was still inflexible, and unfortunately there was no appeal, as the captain had turned in for the night. On getting back to the hotel, Gerald, who did not relish going to bed only to have to turn out again at daybreak, said he would go and tackle the steward. How the great man was conciliated I know not, but after some demur he agreed to prepare berths for Gerald and 'a friend.' When he saw who the

SKYE.

'friend' was, for Gerald had acknowledged no connection with me, his indignation was so evident that he deemed it wisest to retire to his pantry. I thought me of the laws of the

Medes and Persians, but was merciful and said nothing. However, the autocrat of the stateroom was fully revenged, for a wretched steam-crane began to work about midnight, and sleep was impossible.

The discharging and lading of goods at night is one great objection to the stopping steamers which run between Glasgow and Stornoway, otherwise the trip for those who have plenty of time at their disposal is a pleasant one. The shortest sea-route is from Strome Ferry to Stornoway, but it necessitates a most tedious railway journey. Perhaps the best plan is to join the Liverpool-Stornoway boat at Oban, and sail thence without stoppage to Lewis.

In the small hours of the morning Vernon and the rest of our party came on board, and we steamed out of the harbour on to a calm sea, heading for Skye, and bound for Oban and civilisation. As we cleared the Eye of Lewis, Broad Bay opened out, but Gheira Lodge was hidden in the dusk of early morn. The dark mountains of Harris were just visible, but long before we arrived in sight of the mainland a Scotch mist began to fall, hiding all distant things, and we had seen the last of peat-scented Thule.

'BOUND FOR OBAN AND CIVILISATION.

Edinburgh: T. and A. CONSTABLE
Printers to Her Majesty

www.ingramcontent.com/pod-product-compliance
Lightning Source LLC
Chambersburg PA
CBHW020928230426
43666CB00008B/1618